HITCHCOCKTAILS

HITCHCOCKTAILS

LETHAL LIBATIONS INSPIRED BY
THE MASTER OF SUSPENSE

LAURENCE MASLON

Cocktail Photography by Joan Marcus

weldon**owen**

In a promotional still for his immensely successful television anthology series, Alfred Hitchcock serves up a killer cocktail.

CONTENTS

INTRODUCTION • 7

•

WRONG PLACE, WRONG TIME • 14

The Man Who Knew Too Much (1934) • The 39 Steps • Stage Fright
The Wrong Man • North By Northwest • The Birds • Frenzy

I SPY • 36

Secret Agent • Foreign Correspondent • Saboteur • Rear Window
The Man Who Knew Too Much (1956) • Torn Curtain

UNDER YOUR SKIN • 56

Sabotage • The Lady Vanishes • Spellbound
Rope • Strangers on a Train • Psycho

FOREIGN CLIMES • 78

Lifeboat • Under Capricorn • I Confess • To Catch a Thief
The Trouble with Harry • Topaz

ICE MAIDENS • 98

Rebecca • Mr. and Mrs. Smith • The Paradine Case
Dial M for Murder • Vertigo • Marnie

NAME YOUR POISON • 118

Suspicion • Shadow of a Doubt • Notorious • Family Plot

•

LIST OF DRINKS BY MAIN INGREDIENT • 140

ACKNOWLEDGMENTS • 142

ABOUT THE PHOTOGRAPHER • 142

ABOUT THE AUTHOR • 143

INTRODUCTION

" Give Mr. Kaplan a drink, Leonard."

What could sound more hospitable than that, especially as purred solicitously by James Mason in *North by Northwest*? But in the diabolical hands of Alfred Hitchcock, the hospitable quickly becomes the horrible, as poor Mr. Kaplan—actually Cary Grant, perilously misidentified—is given not only a glass of bourbon but a whole bottle—a chaser toward doom; it's murder by congeniality.

This is the method to Hitchcock's madness: the juxtaposition of conviviality and cruelty, of sociability and sadism, of manners and murder—for one without the other would be meaningless. That's the art of his tension, the tension of his art.

Alfred Hitchcock made forty-three full-length movies and, in every one of his sound pictures, people down an alcoholic beverage—every single one, including one film set on a lifeboat in the middle of the Atlantic Ocean.

Hitchcock himself appreciated good food and drink; he was a gourmand who enjoyed a leisurely lunch at the best hotels and an oenophile who knew his wine and liquor. (When Mel Brooks premiered *High Anxiety*, his 1977 comic compendium of Hitchcock's films, Hitchcock sent him a case of Château Haut-Brion 1961 with a note that read, "What a splendid entertainment. You should have no anxieties of any kind.") Of course, Hitchcock had his own favorite cocktail (see page 73).

But he also knew how well food and drink could be deployed to portray the full range of human behavior and he skillfully used them for his nefarious narrative purposes. Sometimes Hitchcock used real bars and nightclubs for his settings—the Savoy Grill, the 21 Club, the Oak Room at the Plaza. Sometimes it was brandies and sodas in posh Mayfair parlors, sometimes in parlor cars; sometimes Champagne at lavish banquets on the Riviera, sometimes in the privacy of, say, one's Greenwich Village rear apartment. Hitchcock's choices are never random, of course, and he—in collaboration with his production designers—always made sure that the protagonist's bar was perfectly appointed and appropriately stocked. In the days before product placement, you could easily spot when one character kept the frugal Black &

OPPOSITE: On a wing and a prayer: Hitchcock directs some high-flying extras on the set of *The Birds* (1963).
ABOVE: Hitchcock takes a snooze while his wife, Alma Reville (left), chats with his assistant/future screenwriter Joan Harrison and writer Mike Hogan in a Hollywood restaurant during preparations for *Rebecca* (1939).

White Scotch on his bar, while a more upscale character in another film might give a bottle of Johnnie Walker Red pride of place.

Nine times out of ten, when a Hitchcock character is startled, shocked, or shaken—a frequent occurrence—they are offered a glass of brandy to stiffen their resolve. (Appropriately, in the later film *Topaz*, largely set in Paris, they are offered a glass of cognac.) A product of his mid-twentieth-century time and his Anglo-American milieu, Hitchcock traded in the acceptable spirits of his era: brandy, whiskey, gin—maybe bourbon and vodka. It was not uncommon at this time for these reliable liquors to be decanted into cut-crystal bottles with little embossed medallions hung around their necks—as it were—to identify them. Not for Hitchcock the mai tai or the Long Island iced tea; even though he employed umbrellas rather spectacularly during a funeral sequence in *Foreign Correspondent*, they were the real thing, rather than brightly colorful paper brollies garnishing a tropical drink.

Indeed, in most things, Hitchcock, and by extension the idiosyncratic tropes in his films, was a product of his era: paternalistic, privileged, misogynistic, overly respectful of social

constructs and creature comforts. Born six months before the twentieth century began, Hitchcock grew up in comfortable middle-class circumstances in and around London, and by the 1920s, had learned every aspect of the embryonic sound-film game. After helming several well-received British thrillers, he was lured to Hollywood in 1939 and constructed a score of brilliantly assembled films, featuring the most attractive stars (Cary Grant, Ingrid Bergman, Grace Kelly, Jimmy Stewart) of the day. By the late 1950s, Hitchcock had become the world's most famous director—or at least the most easily recognizable director famous for being a director. He became the darling of cineastes and theoretical thinkers all over the globe; he was chuffed, bewildered, and bemused by their attentions. With the invention of television, Hitchcock had also become a *brand* and by the time he passed away in 1980, the next generation had emulated his kind of movies so successfully that it was able, in some ways, to beat him at his own game—a game that he had created with such idiosyncratic originality.

In many ways, the ubiquity of Hitchcock's influence—as well as the general availability of most of his films on DVD and streaming services—served to divert the direction of this particular cocktail book from its initial intentions. Given the playfulness of Hitchcock's sense of humor, it would have

OPPOSITE: Hitchcock directs Cary Grant in a scene from *Suspicion*, with cameraman Harry Stradling (1941).
ABOVE: With Grace Kelly, in her Hitchcock premiere, on the set of *Dial M for Murder*, with its ubiquitous bar behind them (1954).

been entirely appropriate to introduce a series of cocktails with cutie-bootie names, such as "The Man Who Drank Too Much" or "The Trouble with Sherry," but after watching all of Hitchcock's films in order, another design began to coagulate before my eyes, underpinned with a more serious intent.

The vast majority of Hitchcock films are set contemporaneously—there is the occasional, rare period costume drama, sure, but no epic historical biographies. His characters tend to be British or American upper-middle-class people, usually literate and articulate (and nearly always white—although Hitchcock deployed slightly more people of color in his films than most commercial directors of his time), often in conventional and comfortable urban settings, usually with a well-stocked bar in the background. And this means that liquor is nearly always used to structure and lubricate social situations; in *Notorious*, for example, the intrepid Ingrid Bergman is inveigled into Claude Rains's calculating web over martinis in a *haute* restaurant in Rio; likewise, Grace Kelly, in *Rear Window*, attempts to seduce a recalcitrant Jimmy Stewart with a pair of swirling brandy snifters.

So, then, might it not be better to *join* Hitchcock in a cocktail, rather than hold him at a jocular arm's length? Each of the cocktails presented herein has some connection to the imbibing that occurs in the respective film itself, along with some sense of the context in which drinking occurs within the narrative. Given how accessible Hitchcock's films are in the digital age, why not rent/download/stream/purchase one of his classics (they rarely stretch much beyond the two-hour range), pour the ingredients into a shaker, mix, and serve—you'd be surprised how felicitously the drinks and the films go together: the films themselves hold up extremely well and you can hold up your cocktail glass and raise a toast to them!

There are many books available to the reader about all the angles—tangential, technical, and otherwise—in Hitchcock's films: the blondes, the camerawork, the storyboards, the neuroses (director *and* characters), the treatment of actors, the *mis*treatment of actors . . . you get the picture. This book celebrates that tension between conviviality and chaos that lurks at the beating heart of each of his movies and inside every cocktail shaker. Which shall it be, provision or poison, something to take the edge off or something to take your head off?

You might even call these drinks "mixtures of suspense."

"Cheers," as Leonard would say, with a healthy—or is that unhealthy?—cascade of bourbon.

ABOVE: Hitchcock showing Brian Aherne how to balance a glass of scotch, prepping for a shot in *I Confess* with Anne Baxter (1953).

FOLLOWING PAGES: Hitch (hands in pockets) rehearses the entire cast of *Rope* (1948) on the film's versatile set.

WRONG PLACE, WRONG TIME

Vandamm's henchmen (l-r: Adam Williams, Martin Landau, and Robert Ellenstein) set up Roger Thornhill (Cary Grant) for a fall in *North by Northwest* (1959).

It is increasingly a part of the complications of modern times: your identity is taken, mistaken, or stolen. It's upsetting, annoying, and in some deep existential way, unnerving. Now, imagine if someone had mixed up your identity with that of someone who committed a crime—killed someone, say, or had robbed an insurance company—and found you guilty for it? That might cost you your reputation, at least—perhaps your very life.

Hitchcock took this narrative device to its limit. As a young boy, by his own account (perhaps overdramatized?), he once spent a brief episode locked in a police jail cell as a punishment for a minor childhood infraction. His father considered this a valuable lesson and, to the extent that it heightened Hitchcock's appreciation for crime and punishment, it was. Hitchcock also grew up at the dawn of the great British fictional thriller, full of suspense and twists and turns, most often inflicted upon ordinary people in extraordinary circumstances. Hitchcock would master the form, consistently refining his storytelling, constantly setting the bar higher for himself, with technological and structural challenges.

He understood deeply (perhaps as a result of his Jesuit education) that we all have secrets and we're all culpable for something: we usually just get away with it. As Richard Brody, a film critic for the *New Yorker*, wrote about Hitchcock's aptly titled film *The Wrong Man*: "Hitchcock's ultimate point evokes cosmic terror: innocence is merely a trick of paperwork, whereas guilt is the human condition." In most of Hitchcock's cases, this "cosmic terror" transitions into an exponential narrative curve, where the hero and/or heroine finds themselves sinking deeper into the tar pit of unintended consequences the more deeply they struggle to escape.

This is not a new narrative device—think of Jean Valjean being pursued relentlessly by the fixated lawman Javert in *Les Misérables*—nor one exclusive to Hitchcock: think of the TV series and film *The Fugitive*. But Hitchcock turned the device into something more compelling: his "wrong" men and women are as ordinary as the day is long, but their travails require them to be inventive, to exist outside their comfort zone, to collaborate with other people they might abhor. Certainly they deserve a toast for their efforts to clear themselves. And probably they also deserve a good strong drink.

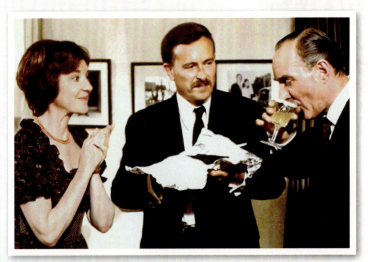

OPPOSITE BELOW: Cordiality among rivals: Bob Lawrence (Leslie Banks, left) and Abbott (Peter Lorre) in *The Man Who Knew Too Much* (1934).

OPPOSITE ABOVE: Elegant smuggler Commodore Gill (Alastair Sim) counsels his daughter Eve (Jane Wyman) and Inspector "Ordinary" Smith (Michael Wilding) in *Stage Fright* (1950).

ABOVE: Melanie (Tippi Hedren) retires to the local bar to show Mitch (Rod Taylor) where she was attacked in *The Birds* (1963).

RIGHT: Sergeant Spearman (Michael Bates) tries Mrs. Oxford's (Vivien Merchant) "te-kweel-a" cocktail, as her husband, Chief Inspector Oxford (Alec McCowen), looks on skeptically, in *Frenzy* (1972).

17

Manny Balestrero (Henry Fonda) retraces his ill-fated steps in *The Wrong Man* (1956).

INSPIRED BY
THE MAN WHO KNEW TOO MUCH (1934)

GIN AND FRENCH

When, after kidnapping your child and then giving you a sock on the jaw, Peter Lorre offers you a drink, you'd probably think twice.

In Hitchcock's first assay on this plot (the second version would be in color and for Hollywood), a sophisticated married couple stumbles into a web of international intrigue and their daughter is kidnapped by a terrorist gang as a way of using leverage against them. Lorre, who had made his international reputation as a child murderer in *M*, a German film from 1931, had been lured to London to play the heavy, and Hitchcock was so impressed with Lorre's dimension and subtle portrayal that he promoted him from a gang flunky in the original script to the gang leader.

Hitchcock takes the kidnapping of the child quite seriously and turns it into a gut-wrenching narrative drive. When the girl's father, played by Leslie Banks, seeks to rescue her but winds up playing directly into Lorre's fiendish grip, one fears the worst. But Lorre—settling graciously and easily into the role of suave antagonist—proffers Banks a cigarette and asks him if he wants a drink. "Gin and French," Banks replies.

Events ramp up rather quickly after that, so we're never quite sure whether Banks actually gets his cocktail, but you can.

GLASS LOWBALL

---

2 ounces dry gin (Old Tom Gin is good)

2 ounces sweet vermouth (Dolin or Noilly Prat will call it "rouge"—as long as it's French)

1 substantial lemon peel

With some generous ice, pour equal measures of gin and vermouth; stir gently. Strain into a lowball or cordial glass. Add the lemon peel.

Bob Lawrence (Leslie Banks, right) does what he needs to do in order to rescue his kidnapped daughter.

20 | WRONG PLACE, WRONG TIME

ABOVE: Hannay (Robert Donat) unravels the mystery of the 39 steps in this lobby card from the movie.

RIGHT: Pamela (Madeleine Carroll) is given a lesson in discretion by Hannay.

INSPIRED BY
***THE 39 STEPS* (1935)**

ALT-NA-SHELLACH

Despite visiting from Canada, Richard Hannay has all the hallmarks of a dashing British hero: a trim moustache, a way with women, the easy deployment of a witty riposte, and—most important for this film—a spontaneous and clever way of thinking on his feet. And he also has an elegantly appointed bar in his apartment—all burnished mahogany and mirrored backsplash—which proves to be particularly useful when he pours a drink for a beautiful and enigmatic spy late one night . . .

The 39 Steps is widely considered the first movie where Hitchcock launches all his characteristic rockets in the same direction. Indeed, the film contains mistaken identity, a man on the run, railway trains, a delicious tension between the sexes, an ingenious solution to a mystery hidden in plain sight, and chases, chases, chases.

One of these chases sends Hannay to the Highlands of Scotland, to an estate called "Alt-Na-Shellach," where he barges into a cocktail party thrown by a suave operator known as "the Professor" who genially offers Hannay "a few drinks to celebrate my daughter's birthday." The scene also surely provides the first appearance of one of the most frequently employed lines in the history of movies: "You leave me no alternative." This is proffered by the Professor gently before, well, choosing an unfortunate alternative.

This cocktail, based on the kind of single malt Scotch whiskey found in the Highlands, leaves you no real alternatives either.

GLASS LOWBALL (A NICE, THICK, ETCHED ONE WOULD BE APPROPRIATE)

½ ounce ruby port

1 large ice cube

2½ ounces single malt Scotch whisky (I'm fond of Glenfarclas–nothing too smoky)

Branch of lavender

Pour the port into a lowball glass, then add a large ice cube, then the Scotch whisky. Go to your local florist or plant shop and get a little lavender plant and use a branch to gently stir the cocktail: it needn't be entirely blended—just enough to get the separate tastes to emerge.

INSPIRED BY
STAGE FRIGHT (1950)

LOVELY DUCKS

Perhaps it's the return to a London venue that brings so much playfulness out of Hitchcock, or maybe it's the acting ensemble he hired for this comedy-thriller. There's Hollywood's Jane Wyman; the scene-stealing Alastair Sim, as Wyman's wily dad; and Marlene Dietrich as the self-absorbed star. Dietrich makes this movie a real hoot, whether she's warbling a Cole Porter ditty written expressly for her or dispensing one-liners in a manner drier than vermouth.

The cocktail for this film comes from yet another eccentric cameo, that of Joyce Grenfell. Grenfell, a much-beloved British comedienne, runs a charity booth for the Theatrical Garden Party where able marksmen can "shoot lovely ducks and win some lovely prizes!" Grenfell's unselfconscious enthusiasm for the rewards—personal and proprietary—of her shooting gallery has just the right kind of theatrical lunacy for this picture: lovely, indeed.

GLASS CHAMPAGNE COUPE
(AS WIDE AS POSSIBLE)

1 ounce dry gin

1 ounce Triple Sec or orange curaçao

1 ounce blue curaçao (or two dashes of blue curaçao syrup)

½ ounce lemon juice

Dash of orange bitters

Ice

Tonic water or mineral water

In a shaker, mix the gin, Triple Sec, curaçao, lemon juice, bitters, and ice. Shake and strain into the coupe. Then add some fizzy water as a floater on top. And of course as many lovely ducks as you can fit! (Easily available online; I like the yellow ones, because I'm old-fashioned.)

Diva Charlotte Inwood (Marlene Dietrich) gives struggling actress Eve Gill (Jane Wyman) some tips about star quality.

24 | WRONG PLACE, WRONG TIME

INSPIRED BY
THE WRONG MAN (1956)

THE STORK CLUB COCKTAIL

It wouldn't be unreasonable to describe this entry as a "film noir": certainly, its grim, gritty, and angular New York location makes *The Wrong Man* part of a continuum of movies from *The Naked City* to *Sweet Smell of Success* that portray the morally ambiguous underbelly of New York's urban landscape. Hitchcock was inspired by the true story of Christopher "Manny" Balestrero, a bass player at New York's fabled Stork Club, who was erroneously charged with a robbery and spent many years (and, as the movie points out piteously, countless dollars) maintaining his innocence. Hitchcock and his technical team do an amazing job following Henry Fonda (as Balestrero) in near-documentary form through the lower-middle-class haunts of Jackson Heights, Queens, in the mid-1950s.

Several brief Manhattan sequences are filmed in the actual Stork Club on West 53rd Street. Its bon vivant proprietor was named Sherman Billingsley and he kept a tight rein on its tony clientele: "The Stork Club discriminates against everybody," said columnist Walter Winchell, an habitué. "But if your skin is green and you're rich and famous or you're syndicated, you'll be welcome at the club." Billingsley nonetheless allowed Hitchcock's crew access to the place—something that he apparently never did for any other filmmaker—and that gives *The Wrong Man* yet another level of verité for its cinematic flavor.

Speaking of flavor, although the Stork Club went out of business in 1965, here's its proprietary cocktail.

GLASS MARTINI OR COUPE

1½ ounces gin (Hayman's Old Tom)

Juice of ½ orange (or ½ ounce orange juice)

1 teaspoon lime juice

1 teaspoon Cointreau

Dash of Angostura bitters

Ice

Orange slice or peel

Chill the glass by filling it with water and placing it in the freezer for 5 minutes, then take it out and discard the water. Add the gin, orange juice, lime juice, Cointreau, and bitters to a shaker with ice and shake lightly until cold. Strain into the prepared glass. Garnish with an orange slice or peel.

Rose and Manny Balestrero (Vera Miles and Henry Fonda) outside of Manhattan's Stork Club.

INSPIRED BY
NORTH BY NORTHWEST (1959)

THE RUSHMORE

North by Northwest begins with our hero en route to the Oak Bar in the Plaza Hotel for a couple of martinis. Cary Grant plays Roger O. Thornhill (at least that what he keeps insisting), a canny advertising executive who steps inadvertently into deception, disguises, and derring-do: a Mad Man pursued by madmen.

The plot of *North by Northwest* is a highly logical corkscrew put together by Hitchcock and screenwriter Ernest Lehman and one can actually chart the course of its improbable peregrinations through its many libations. Grant begins with the promise of a martini on Central Park South—which he never gets to drink; he's then nearly drowned to death at the bottom of a bottle of bourbon on Long Island's Gold Coast; he bounces back by sharing a Gibson with the enticing Eva Marie Saint on the Twentieth Century Limited, as it chugs north along the Hudson; he affects a tenuous rapprochement over a Scotch—no ice—at Chicago's Ambassador Hotel; and he gets to disrupt the villain's celebratory Champagne toast in the shadow of Mt. Rushmore.

Easily one of Hitchcock's most enjoyable and unpredictable films, *North by Northwest*'s luster is only dimmed slightly by the reflected effortfulness of its many, many imitators. It is such a full bar of movie delights that one can only concur with Thornhill (or is that Kaplan?) when offered a lethal dose of bourbon by Martin Landau's saturnine bodyguard, Leonard: "I've had enough stimulation for one day."

As Leonard says in response: "Cheers."

GLASS CHAMPAGNE FLUTE

½ ounce Nux Alpina Walnut liqueur
2½ ounces Champagne, chilled
Dash of orange bitters
Orange peel

Pour the liqueur into a Champagne flute, top off with the Champagne, then add the bitters. Garnish with an orange peel.

Thornhill (Cary Grant) and Eve (Eva Marie Saint) are in a tight spot on Mount Rushmore.

28 | WRONG PLACE, WRONG TIME

INSPIRED BY
NORTH BY NORTHWEST (1959)

GEORGE KAPLAN

In the film, the henchmen of Vandamm (James Mason) get Cary Grant so drunk on bourbon that they hope he'll crash in a fatal car accident. Although the scene is set on Long Island's Gold Coast (and the location of Vandamm's "mansion" is the former Phipps estate in Westbury, Long Island), the treacherous highways and byways were actually filmed along the California coastline. By all accounts, this cocktail should be a lethal libation served out of a bottle, but, gentlemen—let's be reasonable.

GLASS LOWBALL

2 ounces bourbon
1 ounce Tuaca
Dash of orange juice
Ice
Orange peel

Place all the liquid ingredients in a cocktail shaker with ice; shake and strain into a lowball glass. Garnish with an orange peel. Don't get behind the wheel of a car.

THE GIBSON

The basic dry martini (gin, vermouth, bitters) was given a twist, as it were, back at the turn of the twentieth century when members of San Francisco's Bohemian Club omitted the bitters and added a pickled onion instead. Cary Grant's Roger O. Thornhill—an eminently "clubbable" fellow—might well have made this his preferred martini of choice; the Gibson enjoyed its vogue from the 1920s through the 1950s.

GLASS MARTINI OR COUPE

2½ ounces vodka
½ ounce dry vermouth
Ice
Cocktail onion, on a toothpick

Add the vodka, vermouth, and ice to a shaker, shake gently, and strain into a martini glass. Add a cocktail onion. This is a classic cocktail.

ABOVE: Thornhill (Cary Grant) does his best to stay sober—and alive—behind the wheel.

LEFT: Thornhill and Eve (Cary Grant and Eva Marie Saint) share a tense rapprochement over a Scotch in a Chicago hotel room.

INSPIRED BY
THE BIRDS (1963)

LA PALOMA

Watching *The Birds* in a post-pandemic world provides a viewing experience that flies in the face of some criticism leveled against Hitchcock back in the day for not giving us the *motivation* behind these errant and irrational attacks on humanity. However, the director knew it was scarier not to have a know-it-all character propound with some specious rationale; inexplicable gnawing anxiety sometimes works very well for a thriller.

What the movie provides is a bird's-eye view of survival and unlikely alliances in unlikely places. Our flighty heroine (Melanie, played by Tippi Hedren) must, under stressful circumstances, bond with Annie (Suzanne Pleshette); they are both circling around the same man but have to join forces—and of course a bottle of brandy seals the deal of an unlikely friendship. Likewise, at The Tides (the local bar in Northern California's Bodega Bay, re-created bottle by bottle on a soundstage in Hollywood), the local drunk, who asks for Scotch (light on the water), rails against the injustice of the avian Armageddon; he himself is undone by an even more potent octane than Scotch, thanks—if that's the word—to some infernal seagulls.

La Paloma has become a popular drink in recent years. Its West Coast provenance fits in well with Bodega Bay, as does its meaning: *la paloma* is Spanish for "dove." Surely after the sequential ravages of *The Birds*, one would far prefer a peaceful bird to land on—or to land on *you*.

GLASS HIGHBALL

Ice

2 ounces grapefruit soda (Jarritos or Spindrift, which is less sweet)

2 ounces tequila

1 teaspoon lime juice

Grapefruit slice

Place some ice in a highball glass. Pour in the soda, then the tequila and lime juice, and stir slowly; garnish with a grapefruit slice.

A lobby card showing that even schoolchildren aren't immune to the avian wrath in *The Birds*.

INSPIRED BY
FRENZY (1972)

MRS. OXFORD'S MARGARITA

Aficionados welcomed Hitchcock's return to London in this ingeniously constructed "wrong man" trope braided with the ferocious narrative of a serial killer on the loose; indeed, the killer himself makes his home in the environs of the Covent Garden markets where Hitchcock grew up. There's a gritty, tactile quality to the film—a no-nonsense approach to the ramifications of sexual assault and violence. *Frenzy*, even now, let alone in the context of its time—the post–Production Code permissive era of the early 1970s—is not for the faint of heart.

Still, if there were ever a Hitchcock film that invited the viewer to tie one on, it's *Frenzy*. The wronged man, Richard Blaney (played by Jon Finch), has his own dissolute attraction to alcohol and is not above cadging a brandy or three at the pub where he works or sticking his ex-wife with the liquor tab after dinner. But when it comes to the fine art of eating and drinking, that falls to two supporting characters: Chief Inspector Oxford of Scotland Yard and his eccentric wife, who spends her free time in the kitchen experimenting in *haute cuisine*—but her concoctions turn out to be nearly as gruesome (at least to the chief inspector's taste) as the crimes he's pursuing. Mrs. Oxford's recipe for a margarita—not quite as common a menu item back in the 1970s—is nearly as eccentric as she is; she pronounces one ingredient, enthusiastically, as "te-*kweel*-a." Still, it's a full-throated endorsement.

GLASS MARGARITA

Kosher salt

Lemon wedge

2 ounces tequila (pronounced however you like)

1 ounce Triple Sec or Cointreau

1 ounce lemon juice (Mrs. Oxford's idea, not mine)

Ice

Pour some kosher salt onto a small plate. Wet the rim of the cocktail glass with the lemon wedge, then turn it in the salt to coat. Add the tequila, Triple Sec, lemon juice, and ice to a cocktail shaker, shake gently, and pour.

I SPY

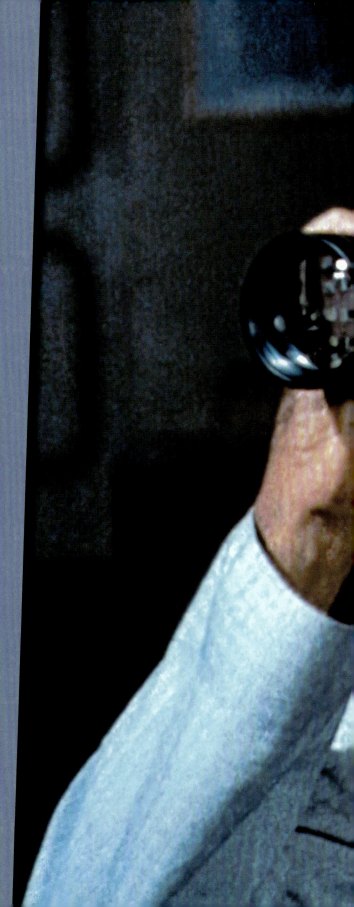

Photographer L. B. Jefferies (James Stewart) doing his visual version of eavesdropping from *Rear Window* (1954).

Alfred Hitchcock grew up in a most interesting time: the first two decades of the twentieth century. To be an adolescent during the Great War, especially in London, where death and destruction were often daily disruptions, was a markedly influential coming-of-age experience.

The international machinations of the Great War gave rise to a burgeoning new genre: the espionage story. By all accounts, the young Hitchcock devoured them. For a young lad growing up in London, there were magazine stories and short books to be had by Joseph Conrad, John Buchan, "Sapper"'s suspense hero, Bulldog Drummond, and eventually, W. Somerset Maugham, all of whom Hitchcock would engage with in one way or another as a director. *Sabotage* was based on Conrad's *The Secret Agent* and—somewhat confusingly— the film *Secret Agent* was "inspired," one might say, rather than "adapted," from two Maugham stories about a British government agent named Ashenden.

Nearly every trope from every spy film into the 1960s originated in a Hitchcock espionage film. *Secret Agent* utilizes a fake-out opening to introduce the hero's identity, a trick used not once but twice in various James Bond movies. And in the same film, the ensemble cast is deployed to provide one of the very first "team-up" movies, where a complementary, but vastly variegated quartet of spies teams up, in this case, to prevent some essential British military plans from falling into (discreetly unnamed) foreign hands.

By the mid-1940s, Hitchcock could turn his attention to the Cold War and its potential atomic confrontations. In fact, *Notorious* bids fair to be the first ur-James Bond film, with its secret agents, secret service, seductive damsel, exotic locale, suave villain, and nuclear secrets. Between *Notorious* and *North by Northwest*, the narrative runway was cleared for every Bond film from *Dr. No* and beyond (Cary Grant—having already broken trail in the spy business—was offered the part of Bond but declined to be part of a franchise).

The closest Hitchcock may have come to Bond was his casting of Sean Connery in *Marnie*, but by the mid-1960s, it would be difficult, if not impossible, to treat an espionage picture—after films such as *Dr. No*, *Fail Safe*, *Dr. Strangelove*, and so many more—with the same kind of insouciance that Hitchcock displayed in his early spy pictures. It was a case of Hitchcock creating an entire genre from scratch—and then watching the world grow so complex and sophisticated that it left his lighthearted touch behind.

OPPOSITE: A much-needed drink after a hair-raising chase: Elsa (Madeleine Carroll), Ashenden (John Gielgud), and The General (Peter Lorre) in *Secret Agent* (1936).

TOP: A distraught mother (Doris Day) is given a strong sedative by her husband (James Stewart) in the 1956 remake of *The Man Who Knew Too Much*.

RIGHT: Scientist Michael Armstrong (Paul Newman) and his assistant– and fiancée–Sarah Sherman (Julie Andrews) have a heated discussion over Cold War politics in *Torn Curtain* (1966).

While the city sleeps—or whatever it does: James Stewart and Grace Kelly as L. B. Jefferies and Lisa Fremont in *Rear Window*.

> **INSPIRED BY**
> **SECRET AGENT (1936)**

THE GENERAL

Secret Agent has all the insolent charm of a brand-new genre—the espionage picture—and Hitchcock takes full advantage of his cinematic palette to introduce some innovations, demonstrating how a spy story could play more thrillingly as a film than on the printed page.

Hitchcock had wanted Robert Donat and Madeleine Carroll to reprise their tag-team escapades from *The 39 Steps* as a pair of spies pretending to be married so they could carry out the orders of His Majesty's Secret Service, but Donat had other commitments. Carroll inherited a part with more, well, agency and a new leading man, John Gielgud, who was the reigning classical star of the British theater but had close to zero film experience.

They were supported by two actors on loan from Hollywood: Robert Young and Peter Lorre. Young was thrilled to work with Hitchcock, especially after his usual "guy-who-doesn't-get-the-girl" roles. Lorre reteamed with the director two years after *The Man Who Knew Too Much* to play "The General," a seemingly polysexual assassin with a passion for a whiskey flask. Referred to as a "hairless Mexican," Lorre is neither hairless (he was coiffed every morning for hours by studio hairdressers) nor Mexican, as his Hungarian accent clearly attests. In a film where nothing—not even the villain(s)—is/are quite what they seem, this is entirely appropriate.

GLASS LOWBALL

Hungarian paprika

Lime wedge

2 ounces tequila

2 ounces Nixta, a Mexican corn liqueur

Juice of ½ lime

Ice

Sprinkle a generous amount of paprika on a small plate. Using the lime wedge, rim the edge of the glass and twirl the wet edge in the paprika. In a cocktail shaker, add the tequila, Nixta, lime juice, and ice. Shake and strain into the prepared glass.

OPPOSITE: Peter Lorre flew back from his nascent Hollywood career to work with Hitchcock again in *Secret Agent*.

ABOVE: A treacherous assignment interrupts a dinner in Switzerland for three secret agents (Peter Lorre, Madeleine Carroll, and John Gielgud).

I SPY | 43

INSPIRED BY FOREIGN CORRESPONDENT (1940)

THE SAVOY HOTEL COCKTAIL

Two years after Hitchcock headed from London to America, he helmed an espionage picture about an American who goes to London. Of course, within those two years, much had changed. As one agitated newspaper editor in the film says about the widening shadow of war, "It's the biggest story in the world today."

The editor, ensconced in the offices of the *New York Morning Globe* (a dead ringer for the *Daily Planet*, by the way), hires his most combative reporter (charmingly played by Joel McCrea) to get a real story from the front lines of Europe. In the course of his escapades, the reporter transforms from an ink-stained hack into an action hero. George Sanders is there for moral and espionage support as a fellow named Ffolliott, a kind of early Felix Leiter.

The writer Robert Benchley, of Algonquin Round Table fame, joins them in the small part of an American journalist regretfully on the wagon ("It's that—or a new set of organs"). The fabled Savoy Hotel provides the setting for an international peace conference, where the cocktails are overflowing. When stumped by a Latvian diplomat who knows no English, McCrea's character foists a martini into his hand: "[This is] the universal language—now we're getting somewhere."

GLASS LIQUEUR GLASS

1 ounce crème de cacao

1 ounce Bénédictine

1 ounce brandy

As the 1930 *Savoy Hotel Cocktail Book* instructs: "Pour ingredients separately and carefully so that do they not mix."

Newspaper reporter Johnny Jones (Joel McCrea) discovers his adventuresome nature trying to rescue kidnapped diplomat Van Meer (Albert Bassermann).

INSPIRED BY
FOREIGN CORRESPONDENT (1940)

CLAUSE 27

The object of the increasingly entangling espionage in *Foreign Correspondent* is an esteemed Dutch pacifist named Van Meer, played by German actor Albert Bassermann. Bassermann himself was also an esteemed figure—a highly regarded stage and film actor throughout Europe who, in a harbinger of the film's conflict, had emigrated from Germany in 1939 to protect his Jewish wife from the Nazis. At the age of 73, he began a new career in Hollywood and apparently learned all his dialogue in *Foreign Correspondent* phonetically (perhaps accounting for his halting but genteel line readings); nevertheless, his performance as Van Meer was key to the picture's success and Bassermann was nominated for a Best Supporting Actor Oscar.

The Clause 27 is based on Van Meer's secret clause to initiate a peace treaty among the Allied and Axis powers. Given Van Meer's nationality—Dutch—the people who originated gin (*genever*), we choose one of the few Dutch gins on the market and mix it with a French vermouth and a German liqueur, hoping the elements will blend harmoniously.

GLASS COUPE

2 ounces Zuidam gin
1 ounce Jägermeister liqueur
1 ounce Dolin blanc vermouth
Ice
Brandied cherry

In a shaker, mix the liquid ingredients and ice, then strain into a coupe. Garnish with a brandied cherry.

In Amsterdam, an assassin escapes in the rain.

INSPIRED BY
SABOTEUR (1942)

ROUTE 66

With the advent of America's involvement in World War II, spies and sabotage were no longer theoretical concerns, they were real anxieties on the national home front, so Hitchcock recomposed *The 39 Steps* on an American canvas: he sends his hero (Barry Kane, played by Robert Cummings) on a cross-country chase to prove his innocence, from the factory floors of California to the landmarks of New York City.

With so much traveling—there are cars, cabs, trucks, trains (a fantastic traveling circus with its own cast of characters within a cast of characters)—there is also the opportunity to sample any number of drinks. Kane is offered a cocktail during his first encounter with a shady character—a Hitchcock trope appearing in its first American context—the elegant ranch owner Charles Tobin, played by the supremely oily Otto Kruger. Farther east, a luxurious cocktail reception in Manhattan seems to disguise some other nefarious goings-on. The film makes brilliant use of three legendary New York City settings: Radio City Music Hall, the Brooklyn Navy Yard, and the Statue of Liberty. But for drinking aficionados, perhaps nothing is as amusing as the remote, absurdly desolate Western town that bubbles up in the middle of the movie: Soda City. This recipe includes some cross-continental ingredients; travel safely.

GLASS LOWBALL

1 ounce orange juice

2 ounces Canada Dry ginger ale

1 ounce Fort Hamilton rye, a distillery based in Brooklyn

Dash of grenadine syrup

Ice

In a lowball glass, pour the dash of grenadine. In a cocktail shaker, add orange juice and rye with ice. Shake and pour with ice into the glass, then add ginger ale to taste.

Accused saboteur Barry Kane (Robert Cummings) and companion Pat Martin (Priscilla Lane) on the trail of the real saboteur find themselves in Soda City.

INSPIRED BY
REAR WINDOW (1954)

MISS LONELYHEARTS

Film fans and students of cinematic technique go cuckoo for Cocoa Puffs over Hitchcock's multilayered tour de force of framing and voyeurism, but don't let the semiotics crowd overcomplicate the movie's delightful combination of suspense, sexuality, and humor.

Grace Kelly makes her Hitchcock debut in this picture, as the most desirable debutante in Manhattan history, adorned in Edith Head's exquisite frocks. She spends an awful lot of time plying Jimmy Stewart's invalid photographer with various kinds of liquor—Champagne, a bottle of Montrachet—in order to melt his incomprehensible resistance to her charms. At one point, she holds two full brandy snifters in front of her torso, like a kind of crystal brassiere.

You wouldn't think that a film set almost entirely within one Greenwich Village apartment would contain so much drinking, but Stewart's intrusive camera lens exposes a lot of secrets belonging to a lot of people. This cocktail is inspired by the trajectory of another unrequited lover, the desperate Miss Lonelyhearts, a single woman spied upon in various stages of despair. During the film, she makes a pretend date in her apartment with a glass of wine, slugs back some bourbon, staggers off to a nearby bar, and makes a disastrous assignation with a drunken pickup. Here's a toast to Miss Lonelyhearts—and all best hopes for a happy ending, at least as far as one can spy from afar.

GLASS MARTINI OR LIQUEUR

2 ounces bourbon
1 ounce Dubonnet rouge
Dash of Toasted Almond bitters
Ice
Lemon peel

In a cocktail shaker, add the bourbon, Dubonnet rouge, and bitters. Add ice, then shake and strain into a martini glass. Garnish with a lemon peel.

OPPOSITE: Judith Evelyn, as the character dubbed "Miss Lonelyhearts," steels herself for an assignation.

ABOVE: A cocktail party viewed through the *Rear Window*: the party host is played by actor Ross Bagdasarian, who gave the world *Alvin and the Chipmunks*. Hitchcock makes a cameo as his butler.

> **INSPIRED BY**
> **THE MAN WHO KNEW TOO MUCH (1956)**

QUE SERA

Hitchcock fans constantly wrangle over which version of this title is better: the crazy, loopy, intense black-and-white version or the one with Doris Day. Anyone who underestimates Doris Day—or her character, Jo McKenna—does so at their peril. As a mother existentially desperate with worry when her son is kidnapped, Day is prepared to do anything to bring him home safely—even sing "Que Sera, Sera." (Written expressly for the film by Jay Livingston and Ray Evans, the song won the Academy Award and became Day's signature song.)

Due to the fact that the first half of the film is set in Marrakesh, there isn't a lot of consumption of alcohol—except for a very intense scene where Jimmy Stewart, as Day's physician husband, attempts to calm her down with some booze and a tranquilizer or two. Once the couple arrives in London, their hotel room comes under siege from a group of well-wishers who seem to drain the resources of the swank hotel's room service in its entirety. One of the entourage swimming around bottles of gin is a young Carolyn Jones (Morticia Addams). The entourage is a bit of a running joke, but they provide the context for one of the best—and most relieved—curtain lines in all of Hitchcock's films.

The Que Sera deploys aspects of both of the film's locations—a little bit of Morocco, a little bit of England. One can only hope the imbiber will enjoy it; the future's not ours to see.

GLASS COUPE

1 ounce Spanish sherry (Pedro Ximinez or something comparatively sweet)

1 ounce Pink Gin

1½ teaspoons El Guapo Creole Orgeat syrup

4 dashes cardamom bitters

Ice

Add sherry, gin, orgeat syrup, bitters and ice into a cocktail shaker. Shake, then strain into a coupe.

Jo McKenna (Doris Day) attempting to solve a particularly gnawing mystery at London's Royal Albert Hall.

> **INSPIRED BY**
> ***TORN CURTAIN* (1966)**

THE TIVOLINI

The plot of *Torn Curtain* revolves around an act of perceived international betrayal—the defection of a high-profile Westerner to the Soviet bloc (it usually happened the other way around during the Cold War). As a brilliant physicist and his equally resourceful fiancée, Paul Newman and Julie Andrews make an intriguing but somewhat uncomfortable couple, perhaps the result of their very different acting backgrounds and some undercooked character developments in the screenplay. *Torn Curtain* allows us a variety of European locations—both in front of and behind the Iron Curtain (hence the title), as well as a climatic event behind a theatrical curtain.

Even with an overloaded buffet of dangerous encounters, *Torn Curtain* pulls away to reveal several unforgettable sequences—one of the most brutal murders Hitchcock (or anyone) ever filmed and a showdown between the world's two most accomplished nuclear physicists in which two pieces of chalk and a blackboard determine the fate of the world.

The tense discussions between Newman and Andrews about the implications of a defection take place over martinis at Copenhagen's legendary Tivoli Gardens, another example of Hitchcock's use of civility during potentially shattering events.

GLASS MARTINI

Ice

2 ounces vodka

1 ounce aquavit

2 lemon peel twists

Chill two martini glasses for 10 minutes in the freezer. In a shaker, add ice, vodka, and aquavit. Stir and strain into the prepared glasses. Add a twist to each.

Two professors (Paul Newman and Ludwig Donath) plot the course of nuclear destruction on a chalkboard.

I SPY | 55

UNDER YOUR SKIN

The psychoanalytic genius Dr. Brulov (Michael Chekhov) and his prized pupil Dr. Constance Petersen (Ingrid Bergman) try to get inside the subconscious of Dr. Anthony Edwardes (Gregory Peck) in *Spellbound* (1945).

To be a British youngster and to discover the American short stories of Edgar Allan Poe must have been a shock; Poe's mastery of dread and coincidence in his tales of obsession, murder, projection, and pathology were unlike anything to be encountered in the English school system's curriculum. Hitchcock took to Poe's oeuvre as a young man and, clearly, it had a profound impact on his own psychology.

Once Hitchcock immigrated to Poe's own country in 1939, he was able—within the confines of the heavily regulated studio system—to inject Hollywood movies with the most potent expressions of the psychological thriller, another genre that he pretty much created out of whole cloth. In this, he was abetted by another visitor from Europe to America: Sigmund Freud, who (along with Carl Jung) gave a series of lectures about psychoanalysis and the subconscious in Worchester, Massachusetts, in 1909. From that moment on, the unmapped terrain of the psyche became a fascination for Americans and by the 1920s, psychoanalysis had become a pastime of the urban elite and a hazy concept for mainstream Americans who only vaguely understood its manifold mysteries.

But this worked to the advantage of Hitchcock and screenwriter Ben Hecht for their first collaboration, *Spellbound*. The duo reached out to various doctors and therapists (including Hecht's own) to vet their script, but they selectively chose a dog's dinner of jargon

Three girlfriends (l-r: Googie Withers, Margaret Lockwood, and Sally Stewart) make the best out of a layover in Madrika in *The Lady Vanishes* (1938).

LEFT: Whatever gets you through the night: Marion Crane (Janet Leigh) consumes a modest repast in the parlor of the Bates Motel in *Psycho* (1960).

ABOVE: Guy Haines (Farley Granger) raises a glass to Barbara (Patricia Hitchcock, the director's daughter) for getting him out of a tight spot in *Strangers on a Train* (1951).

and concepts that made little clinical sense; that's okay, they were provocative enough to provide a premise for a thriller. By the time the Second World War concluded, the year of *Spellbound*'s release, most Americans were a little less naive on the subject, as every serviceman had been given a psychological examination upon induction.

The 1950s brought Hitchcock into contact with two major masters of the psychological thriller with *Strangers on a Train*; it was based on a book by Patricia Highsmith and the screen-play was worked on by Raymond Chandler (although he apparently treated the entire creative process with contempt). Hitchcock also introduced audiences to the concept of the serial killer in films such as *Shadow of a Doubt*, *Psycho*, and *Frenzy*. It would seem to be the last possible genre to appeal to audiences, but where would the eventual battalion of slasher films be without Norman Bates to gash a pathway forward? However, in Hitchcock's discreet hands, this slasher film was always a cut above the rest.

Giving them enough rope: Party guests (Joan Chandler and Douglas Dick) chat while Brandon and Phillip (John Dall and Farley Granger) celebrate in *Rope* (1948).

INSPIRED BY
***SABOTAGE* (1936)**

COCK ROBIN

Sabotage may well be Hitchcock's most pitiless film. It focuses on the routine of an urban terrorist, and the violence is not only domestic: the film also climaxes in domestic violence. If anything, this early "ticking bomb" thriller seems more shocking for audiences today than it did nearly a hundred years ago.

Based on a short 1907 novel by Joseph Conrad (called *The Secret Agent*), *Sabotage* deals with an unnamed terrorist organization seeking to undermine security and morale in pre–World War II London. (Good luck with that: the stiff-upper-lip citizens who populate the movie seem like pretty tough cookies.) A love triangle gently unfolds among the terrorist, his trusting wife, and a neighbor who may not be what he seems. In a film that doesn't have a lot of drinking, there is a lovely sequence where the neighbor takes the wife and her far-too-trusting brother to Simpson's (on the Strand and one of London's most cherished restaurants), beginning Hitchcock's inclination to include actual fine dining establishments in his films.

As far as mixologists go, the most accomplished here is "The Professor," who masquerades as a pet-shop owner in order to cover up his real skills: making bombs. (Hence, the Fireball whisky in the cocktail below.) The Professor stocks his cupboard with "tomato sauce" and "strawberry jam"—but don't ask him to mix an actual cocktail for you: he's far more conversant with nitroglycerin than Negronis.

GLASS LOWBALL

2 ounces Fireball Cinnamon Whisky

1 ounce Tuaca

Several drops of Fernet-Branca

Ice

Dash of ground clove

In a cocktail shaker, combine the whisky, Tuaca, and Fernet-Branca with ice; shake and strain into a lowball glass. Add a dash or two of ground cloves on top.

Spencer (John Loder) gives Mrs. Verloc (Sylvia Sidney) a break from her dreary existence with a visit to Simpson's.

INSPIRED BY
THE LADY VANISHES (1938)

TEST MATCH

Although we start in one of those fictitious Mittel-European countries, the real fun of *The Lady Vanishes* begins when the train pulls out the next morning and complications, as the cliché goes, ensue. This "train of fools"—careening unknowingly into cataclysm—carries in various compartments a distracted musicologist, a privileged young lady (about to be married), a married solicitor having an affair with his secretary, a mature and kindly governess, and a pair of stiff-upper-lip British gents determined to get to England to watch their national team take on Australia in the cricket test match at Old Trafford. Soon, they are joined by a brain surgeon, a devious magician, a nun with a penchant for high heels . . . and *then* it gets complicated.

Hitchcock loved trains and loved how constricted they were and yet how runaway they were—a train trip could divert every narrative to the express track. The parlor car offers multiple opportunities for choice beverages (Chartreuse, brandies) and chance encounters. Our British duo—Charters and Caldicott (played by Basil Radford and Naunton Wayne, respectively)—were so spot-on and so endearing that they went on to appear in a number of other films and radio shows; their attempt at replicating a cricket match in the parlor car by using sugar cubes is a highlight.

GLASS COUPE OR MARTINI

2 ounces Pink Gin

1 ounce Italicus Bergamotto aperitif

Dash of lemon bitters

Sugar cube

Ice

Place sugar cube in glass. Add gin, Italicus, bitters, and ice to the shaker, stir, and strain over the sugar cube.

The train passengers (Naunton Wayne, Margaret Lockwood, Dame May Whitty, Michael Redgrave, Basil Radford, and Cecil Parker) keep a collective stiff upper lip.

UNDER YOUR SKIN

INSPIRED BY
THE LADY VANISHES (1938)

VANISHING LADY

The eponymous "lady" of the title is actually a proper mature governess, Miss Froy—although the studio promotional flacks (both in 1938 and for a 1979 remake) attempted to imply that the "lady" was the far more nubile leading actress. In Hitchcock's case, the redoubtable Miss Froy is played by Dame May Whitty—the first British actress to be given the honorific for services to the British Empire during World War I. Whitty's character has her own fondness for drink; in this case, a particular blend of tea called Harriman's. An important plot point; best to make a note of it before it flies by.

GLASS LOWBALL

2 ounces dry gin
1 ounce St Raphael rouge
1 teaspoon chai tea syrup

Frost a glass by rinsing it with water and putting it in the freezer for 30 minutes; in the meantime, combine the ingredients in a cocktail shaker and stir. When the glass is ready, use a cotton swab to write "FROY" on the frosted glass, and strain the drink into it.

Gilbert (Michael Redgrave) seems to ignore the trace of Miss Froy, much to the chagrin of Iris (Margaret Lockwood).

66 | UNDER YOUR SKIN

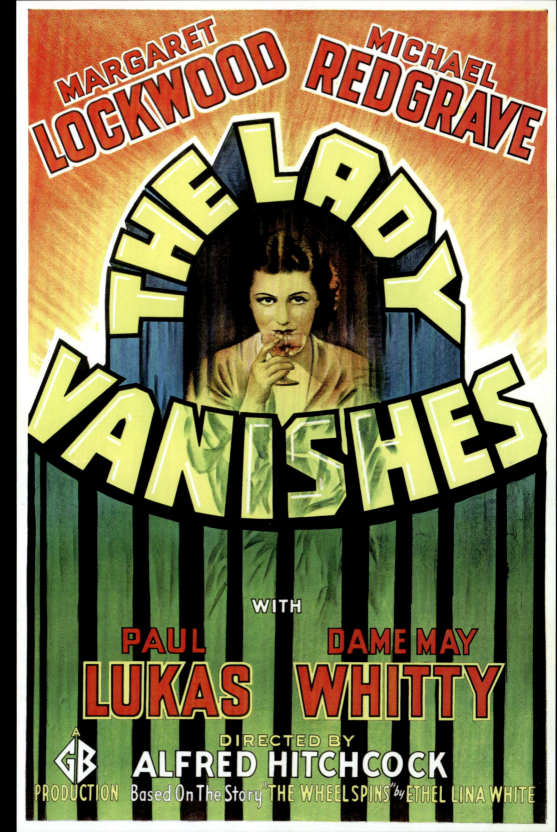

> **INSPIRED BY**
> *SPELLBOUND* (1945)

GABRIEL VALLEY

If *Spellbound* isn't exactly "Freud for Dummies," it certainly presents a fulsome buffet of psychoanalytic jargon for American audiences. In reality, the psychological portrait of the hero, Dr. Edwardes (played stoically by Gregory Peck), probably wouldn't hold any water (or Scotch and water).

The more compelling "spell" is that woven by Ingrid Bergman in her first Hitchcock film. Having arrived in Hollywood from Sweden only five years earlier (this was her tenth film, and she had already won an Oscar), she proved herself capable of holding down a thriller as an adventurous and self-reliant heroine (although she does fall for Peck awfully hard).

The film's alcoholic references include a mild case of sedation and an important clue involving drinks at the 21 Club, a legendary New York speakeasy that transitioned into an elegant restaurant after Prohibition was repealed. (It appears in less-than-realistic form in a dream sequence designed by Salvador Dalí.) And perhaps the real name of Peck's Dr. Edwardes—Ballantyne—is a throw to one of the more popular Scotch whiskies of the day. Of course, that might be a subliminal thought . . .

GLASS MARTINI

2 ounces Scotch

1 ounce amaro (High Wire)

1 ounce lemon juice

Ice

Whipped cream dispenser

4 egg whites

½ ounce simple syrup

Black-colored cake icing

Mix the Scotch, amaro, and ½ ounce of the lemon juice in a cocktail shaker with ice. Using the whipped cream dispenser, make foam using the egg whites, remaining ½ ounce lemon juice, and simple syrup. Dispense foam into a martini glass, then slowly strain in the Scotch mixture. When foam rises to the top, make three parallel lines in the foam with the cake icing to simulate Dr. Edwardes's neurosis.

Even though the scene is shot in a studio, the perils of Gabriel Valley seem very present to Gregory Peck and Ingrid Bergman.

INSPIRED BY
ROPE (1948)

TIED TOGETHER

The first minute of *Rope*'s swift eighty is a murder by strangulation, so that isn't really a spoiler alert, but right after that, Hitchcock's camera focuses on an extremely well-appointed bar in the middle of Brandon Shaw's elegant Manhattan penthouse. Brandon and his partner in crime, Phillip Morgan, share what can only be understood as a postcoital moment, while holding up their victim's last drinking glass, regretting that his final drink would be something as "corrupt as whiskey."

Famously, the camera never leaves the studio set constructed as Brandon's apartment, as Hitchcock attempts to capture the film's nail-biting suspense by shooting the entire movie in one long extended take (due to the technical restrictions of the time, it's actually a series of eight-minute takes streamlined together). Attention to detail is crucial to *Rope*'s cumulative effect—books, paintings, plates, hats, a piano—and a rope, of course—are all given particularly important presences as props, and Brandon's bar is no exception.

For the murderers' secret celebration of their ignominious achievement, a bottle of Veuve Clicquot is brought out: "What would you say to a glass of Champagne?" "Hello, Champagne!" is one character's reasonable retort. Before *Rope* stretches to its conclusion, Brandon's bar will be well utilized; even Jimmy Stewart, as the most sober character in the film, will need a drink—"a long one."

GLASS LOWBALL

2 ounces rye whiskey

1 ounce Chambord or crème de cassis

1 tablespoon curaçao or Triple Sec

1½ teaspoons absinthe

1 egg white

Ice

Put all the ingredients in a shaker, shake, and strain into a lowball glass.

Phillip, Brandon, and their former instructor Rupert (l-r: Farley Granger, John Dall, and James Stewart) are all going to need a stiff drink as tensions tighten.

INSPIRED BY HITCHCOCK'S FILMS

THE CAMEO

Hitchcock himself was no stranger to the cocktail. Indeed, he appreciated the entire gamut of alcoholic options; he was a discerning and copious consumer of wine and reveled in meeting a new screenwriter or producer over a long lunch at, say, Chasen's in Hollywood, a particular favorite watering hole.

Apparently, Hitchcock's preferred cocktail helped buck him up after a career disappointment. In the early 1920s, during his British "internship," he was assigned a film called *Number 13*, which he didn't want to take on. The silent film was unfinished, but a series of cocktails weren't: Hitchcock was so discouraged by the assignment that he went straight to the nearest bar with a chum, saying, "What we need is a White Lady." He knocked them back, according to his pal, "quickly and unfailingly."

The White Lady zoomed along the zinc bar to become one of the most popular cocktails of the 1920s and '30s. The recipe below was made famous at the Savoy Hotel, a favorite London haunt featured in the first part of Hitchcock's 1940 espionage thriller, *Foreign Correspondent*. Some optional recipes feature an egg white added to make the drink frothier; anyone who has seen *Rebecca* with Florence Bates as Mrs. Van Hopper stub out her cigarette into her eggs so peremptorily will have difficulty imagining Hitchcock ordering up *that* version.

GLASS COUPE

---

2 ounces dry gin

1 ounce Cointreau

1 ounce lemon juice

Ice

Add the gin, Cointreau, and lemon juice to a shaker with ice; shake well and strain into a cocktail glass.

OPPOSITE: The Master of Suspense makes an appearance behind Henry Fonda at a late-night New York City eatery in *The Wrong Man*.

INSPIRED BY
STRANGERS ON A TRAIN (1951)

CRISS CROSS

"Here's luck!" toasts Bruno Antony to his companion in the bar car, tennis pro Guy Haines—and worse luck couldn't possibly befall the poor guy. Twelve years after *The Lady Vanishes*, Hitchcock returns to the kind of dramatic chance encounter one can only achieve with traveling companions on a train to destiny. In a handsome, well-appointed bar car from Washington to New York, over a pair of Scotches, Bruno suggests to Guy that he can make a particularly vexatious lady of Guy's acquaintance vanish—permanently. In exchange, that is, for the complementary murder of Bruno's father.

Much of the film's delight is derived from Robert Walker's career-best performance as Bruno, a charming but delusional psychopath who sports a silk tie with a lobster on it: an affluent character with claws. "I've got a theory—you should do everything before you die," he tells Guy (the rather passively earnest Farley Granger), and so he nearly does—at least within the limits of the Production Code.

The Criss Cross is a kind of double game; you'll need a companion—chance or otherwise—to drink it. One glass contains sweet vermouth and gin; the other, dry vermouth and vodka. You first have one round, and then switch the ingredients and have another. You will, as Guy points out, have to drink both of them.

GLASSES MARTINI

DRINK ONE

2 ounces gin

1 ounce sweet vermouth

Ice

Lemon twist

DRINK TWO

2 ounces vodka

1 ounce dry vermouth

Ice

Brandied cherry

To make drink one: Add the gin, sweet vermouth, and ice to a cocktail shaker, shake until cold, then strain into a martini glass and garnish with a lemon twist.

To make drink two: Add the vodka, dry vermouth, and ice to a cocktail shaker, shake until cold, then strain into a martini glass and garnish with a brandied cherry.

For round two, make drink one with vodka and sweet vermouth; and for drink two, switch out the vodka and use gin instead, swapping out the main ingredients for a second round.

Bruno Antony (Robert Walker) stirs up a diabolical dialectic deed for Guy Haines (Farley Granger).

INSPIRED BY
PSYCHO (1960)

A BOY'S BEST FRIEND

Given the legendary mayhem and madness of *Psycho*, a snootful of bourbon would hardly seem to be on the cutting edge of problematic behavior.

Yet one could argue that all of *Psycho*'s travails begin thus: in a dusty little Title and Trust office in Phoenix with a freewheelin' client named Lowery who, after an overindulgent lunch, drunkenly throws around $40,000 in cash. His handsy manner and the potential escape hatch of $40,000 prove to be prime motivators for Marion Crane's quick departure from town—the roads of which lead to the Bates Motel.

Given how well-known this film is—and it was Hitchcock's most commercially successful film, shot with the most modest of means—it's surprising to see how gentle and *accommodating* Norman Bates can be upon meeting Marion Crane; his kind offer of milk and a sandwich seems a far cry from the kind of boozy predator personified by Lowery. Of course, milk and a sandwich is just the kind of repast made by someone who hasn't had, um, a *homecooked* meal in a while.

This cocktail uses preserves—you know, the kind of ingredient that keeps things in the fruit cellar looking . . . *fresh*. It's a bit complicated to make but take a stab at it.

GLASS LOWBALL

2 ounces vodka

1 ounce Blood Orange liqueur

Ice

Dash of Fernet-Branca (or Mr. Black coffee liqueur, if F-B is not to your taste)

Spoonful of Mrs. Bridges blood orange preserves

In a shaker, combine the vodka, blood orange liqueur, and ice; shake. In lowball glass, pour the Fernet-Branca to make sure it coats the bottom, then spoon the preserves so it fills the bottom of the glass. When done, strain the vodka mix into the glass—but do not shake or stir.

A potted customer (Frank Albertson) showers secretary Marion (Janet Leigh) with inappropriate attention at the beginning of *Psycho*.

FOREIGN
CLIMES

Columnist Connie Porter (Tallulah Bankhead), a resourceful lass who's rarely at sea, at the beginning of *Lifeboat* (1944).

Perhaps because he pretty much despised the capriciousness of location shooting, Alfred Hitchcock was a location in himself.

Whether in London or Hollywood, Hitchcock created a universe of his own, surrounding himself with his esteemed technicians, designers, and composers (along, of course, with his beloved wife, collaborator, and sounding board, Alma Reville). He was capable of creating a quaint English village (*Suspicion*) and an exotic Brazilian estate (*Notorious*) in the studio system of Hollywood. This allowed him to have more control over his production schedule and also to break for lunch at the various Los Angeles watering holes that catered to his prodigious appetite.

Political discretion also tamed some of his decisions: in *The Lady Vanishes*, the espionage escapades begin in the fictitious European country of Bandrika, where there is a local inn by the train station; it would not have done to antagonize Germany (or even Italy) in the prewar years. His films from the late 1930s into the '40s were also circumscribed by the limitations of wartime—the Hollywood backlot was the smartest and safest place to be.

By the 1950s, Hitchcock returned to London to capture its quaint theatrical traditions (*Stage Fright*), depicted the evocative Gothic imagery of Quebec City in *I Confess*, and braved the crowds to film in Marrakesh (*The Man Who Knew Too Much*). His command and sweep of the French Riviera locations for *To Catch a Thief* enabled his cinematographer Robert Burks to win an Academy Award, yet the weather conditions in Vermont for *The Trouble with Harry* were so unruly that they sent the director (and Burks) back to Hollywood to re-create the film's autumnal charm in a studio. And while Hitchcock had no trouble filming on locations in Paris and Copenhagen for his 1960s espionage epics, he was smart enough (and obedient enough) to film his Cuban sequences from *Topaz* in Salinas, California.

To watch all of Hitchcock's oeuvre consecutively is to be taken on a worldwide travelogue where his creative use of studio sets and real locations requires only the passport of one's imagination.

A costume ball does little to disguise the dangers as the action comes to a boiling point; Grace Kelly (center).

ABOVE: Milly (Margaret Leighton) tortures the vulnerable Lady Flusky (Ingrid Bergman) in *Under Capricorn* (1949).

BELOW: In *I Confess*, shot on location in the lobby of Quebec City's fabled hotel, the Chateau Frontenac, police inspector Larrue (Karl Malden) cautions Father Logan (Montgomery Clift) to stay out of harm's way.

The artist (John Forsythe) and the twice-widowed neighbor (Shirley MacLaine) share a lemonade in *The Trouble with Harry* (1955).

INSPIRED BY
LIFEBOAT (1944)

THE ROSIE

Hitchcock's conceit of filming an entire narrative while its characters float on a lifeboat in the mid-Atlantic during the height of World War II might seem, on the surface, to be a mere gimmick, but the movie has more to do with human beings and their essential beliefs in civilization than most pictures of a philosophical bent. Part of *Lifeboat*'s success is due to its varied cast of characters: a high society journalist (played magnificently by Tallulah Bankhead), a tetchy working-class crewman, a philosophical millionaire, a jovial seaman from Brooklyn, a Black steward (one of the few Black characters in a Golden Age picture who is given some agency), and so on. "Dying together's even more personal than living together," says one of the survivors. One might think of *Lifeboat* as a comedy of manners under the direst of circumstances: a tragedy of manners.

Cocktails would seem to be the last thing to appear on this rationed menu of existence, but Hitchcock gives us a moment or two on the centrality of drink; a pint of brandy becomes essential to the survival of Gus, the Brooklyn sailor, beautifully embodied in the down-to-earth portrayal of William Bendix.

Gus, injured and delirious from dehydration, dreams of returning in one piece to New York's Roseland Ballroom to cut a rug with his girlfriend, Rosie—an increasing obsession as he is well aware of her other admirers. In honor of Rosie and Roseland, here's the following drink.

GLASS LOWBALL

1 large ice cube

1 ounce Courvoisier

2 ounces Lillet Rosé

2 dashes of El Guapo Rose Water Cordial

Orange peel

In a lowball glass, place the large ice cube, then pour over the Courvoisier. In a shaker, stir the Lillet and the rose water; pour over the ice cube, then garnish with an orange peel. Do not stir.

Joe (Canada Lee, left) negotiates with an untrustworthy passenger Willi (Walter Slezak) in *Lifeboat*.

84 | FOREIGN CLIMES

What you can–and, more importantly, what you cannot–drink at sea becomes an issue between Alice (Mary Anderson) and Gus (William Bendix).

INSPIRED BY
UNDER CAPRICORN (1949)

SHRUNKEN HEAD

Under Capricorn is its own wild capricious Hitchcock cocktail: he took two previous leading actors (Joseph Cotten and Ingrid Bergman, who, at the time, was the world's number one box office attraction) and added an exotic locale (New South Wales in Australia), an ounce of Charlotte Brontë (a Gothic romance set in the early nineteenth century), two dashes of Daphne du Maurier (a forbidding estate and an obsessively jealous housekeeper), and a twist—Bergman plays a rather unsympathetic aristocrat, ravaged by delusion, guilt, and alcoholism.

The resultant film left fervent fans shaken (although the French critics have always extolled its virtues) and stirred controversy (Bergman was involved with an adultery scandal when the movie opened). Nonetheless, *Under Capricorn* has a swirl of images, camera techniques, and performances to intoxicate audiences. (A high society ballroom scene makes one ache to think of what Hitchcock might have done with, say, Thackeray's *Vanity Fair*.) It's certainly the Hitchcock film where the antagonist does the most to undermine the heroine by taking advantage of her isolation, depression, and desire for alcohol. That's where the shrunken heads come in—keep an eye out for one of them early in the film.

"Minyago Yugilla" is the motto for the woebegone Australian estate where most of the action is set: "Why weepest thou?" After a few Shrunken Head cocktails, you may either stop weeping or not give a toss why you started in the first place.

GLASS TIKI MUG

Ice

2 ounces rum (gold)

1 ounce Ponche Pajarote (tamarind liqueur)

1 ounce Cointreau

Juice of ½ lime

1 teaspoon pomegranate molasses

Sprig of mint

In a shaker, put some extra ice and the liquid ingredients; shake vigorously, pour into the tiki mug, and add the mint sprig.

Lord and Lady Flusky (Joseph Cotten and Ingrid Bergman) and Charles Adare (Michael Wilding) get hot under their nineteenth-century collars.

FOREIGN CLIMES | 87

INSPIRED BY
I CONFESS (1953)

THE FRONTENAC

An edgy, angular film about maintaining the dictates of one's conscience against all odds, *I Confess* fits beautifully within the context of the McCarthy era, a morality tale of a Catholic priest who is burdened with a secret that puts him at a crossroads—and in the crosshairs—between ancient duty and contemporary justice.

The movie cleverly crosscuts between Father Logan's simple life among his fellow clerics in his local parish with the sophisticated lifestyle of Quebec City's high society. In one instance, we see Logan rolling up his sleeves to help paint the pantry of his parish; in the next shot, the city's preeminent civil administrator is in the middle of a cocktail party, balancing a Scotch and soda on his head. The cast is particularly fine with Montgomery Clift, who brings sackcloth and ashes to a high art form as the priest; Brian Aherne as the crown prosecutor; Karl Malden as a no-nonsense cop; and Anne Baxter as the femme fatale who is caught in the middle of every iteration of the film's many conundrums.

Hitchcock supposedly didn't quite know how to handle Clift's intense, inner-directed approach to acting, but the actor's personal self-abnegation works extremely well for the character of Father Logan. Besides, Clift eventually gets to display his action hero cred in an extremely tense climax set in Quebec's premier hotel, the glorious Château Frontenac.

GLASS LOWBALL

Ice

2 ounces Canadian Club whisky

1 ounce Calvados

1 tablespoon maple syrup

Dash of orange juice

Orange peel

Pour the ice and liquid ingredients into a shaker. Shake and strain into a lowball glass; garnish with an orange peel.

ABOVE: Quebec City's elite (l-r: Roger Dann, Brian Aherne, and Anne Baxter).

OPPOSITE: A guilt-ridden priest (Montgomery Clift) is questioned by two intractable policemen (Henry Corden, left, and Karl Malden).

INSPIRED BY
TO CATCH A THIEF (1955)

MAQUIS MOUSE

Hitchcock's travelogue tribute to the French Riviera is such a celebratory romp that a bottle of Champagne is featured *in the opening credits.*

Given the film's provincial provenance among high rollers and mischief-makers in Cannes and Monaco, a full range of spirited possibilities would seem obligatory. Gourmet restaurants, casinos, expensive dinners, picnics, and masquerade balls all figure prominently—which means a full complement of Champagne, wine, and cocktails comes for the ride along the Riviera's Moyenne Corniche.

The most potent mixture in this rom-com thriller is one part Cary Grant and one part Grace Kelly, who, when blended, set off such a battery of, um, fireworks that one regrets this was their only film together (although Hitchcock subsequently tried to pair them up again on every possible occasion). The cocktails here, however, are tributes to two other characters. The first is Danielle, an audacious young French woman enamored of Cary Grant (well, I mean . . .). Grant (a retired jewel thief, the Cat), Danielle, and her father and their pals had been members of the Maquis, a French Resistance movement during World War II (and if being a part of the Maquis means being able to pull off Grant's striped sailor shirt and jaunty red ascot, sign me up!). Danielle's underground background is referred to on the hull of her dexterous speedboat.

GLASS CHAMPAGNE FLUTE

½ ounce absinthe or Pernod

Sugar cube

2½ ounces Lillet Rouge

Ice

Pour the absinthe into a Champagne flute and swirl to coat. Place the sugar cube in the glass. In a shaker, add the Lillet and ice; strain into the Champage flute slowly.

Brigitte Auber as Danielle, an alumna of the French Underground, goes underground in *To Catch a Thief*.

FOREIGN CLIMES | 91

INSPIRED BY
TO CATCH A THIEF (1955)

AVEZ-VOUS

The second cocktail inspired by *To Catch a Thief* is a nod to the character of Grace Kelly's mother, an astringent widowed Texas heiress played by Jessie Royce Landis with a double shot of wry. Or rye, as the case may be—for all of the fancy airs of the South of France, Jessie (the character's name, too) would much prefer bourbon and her own backyard: "Bourbon's the only drink. You can pour that champagne down the Channel. Why wait years to drink the stuff? Great vineyards, huge barrels aging forever, poor monks running around testing it, so some woman in Oklahoma can say it tickles her nose!" At the film's climatic exclusive masquerade ball, Jessie asks a bewigged servant, "*Avez-vous* bourbon?"— and who could say "*non*" to her?

GLASS CORDIAL

2½ ounces bourbon
Dash of orange bitters
2 dashes of absinthe or Pernod
Ice
Lemon peel

Add the bourbon, bitters, and absinthe to a shaker, then add ice. Shake and strain into a cordial glass; garnish with a lemon peel.

American tourists Jessie Stevens and her daughter, Frances (Jessie Royce Landis and Grace Kelly), enjoy the high life in Monte Carlo with former burglar John Robie (Cary Grant) and insurance agent Hughson (John Williams).

FOREIGN CLIMES | 93

INSPIRED BY
THE TROUBLE WITH HARRY (1955)

CORPSE REVIVER NO. 8

If there was ever an outlier in the Hitchcock oeuvre, it's the gentle black comedy (would that make it a "gray comedy"?) *The Trouble with Harry*. Some viewers begrudge its simple charms and bucolic setting; perhaps that's because they may have wandered into *Harry*'s world with the wrong expectations: what would you think of, say, *Psycho* if you thought you were going to a screening of *The Apartment*?

Speaking of *The Apartment*, Shirley MacLaine makes her film debut in *Harry* and her off-kilter personality gives the picture its own sense of eccentricity (she surely is one of the most attractive 1950s moms and gives her kid—played, yes, by TV's "Beaver," Jerry Mathers—an awful lot of leeway, especially when she encourages him to play with dead animals). Mildred Natwick and Mildred Dunnock supply depth in supporting roles, and composer Bernard Herrmann's first score for Hitchcock makes an elegiac appearance.

The corpse reviver is a time-honored drink with many variants. I'm not sure it ever made it up to number 8, but here that refers to the number of times of the eponymous Harry's internment (and reinternment), which supplies what parsimonious plot there is at the center of this bucolic movie. The maple syrup addition is a nod to the film's stunning Vermont setting (some of which had to be re-created in the studio).

GLASS MARTINI

½ ounce Lillet Blonde

½ ounce St-Germain elderflower liqueur

½ ounce lemon juice

½ ounce maple syrup

Dash of absinthe

Ice

Pour all the ingredients into a shaker; shake vigorously, and strain into a martini glass.

Arnie (Jerry Mathers) discovers something more disturbing than a ring in the bathtub.

INSPIRED BY
TOPAZ (1969)

THE TOPAZ

This international spy thriller gets a bad rap from Hitchcock fans, and it's not difficult to see why. Based on a complex Leon Uris (*Exodus, QBVII*) novel purportedly foisted on Hitchcock by studio executives, the Cold War espionage film—set during the tense days of the Cuban Missile Crisis—was not helped by a B-level cast of international actors (although the American stage actor Roscoe Lee Browne is delightful as an espionage agent—the largest part played by a Black actor in any of Hitchcock's films) and a plot so complex (and overlong) that Hitchcock filmed three separate endings and left it to the studio to pick one, a kind of cinematic (and fitting) Russian roulette. *Topaz* is more like a very good two-part TV episode of *Mission Impossible*.

Still, the film has much to recommend it: globe-trotting from Denmark to Virginia to Harlem to Cuba to Paris; a luscious Maurice Jarre score; some nail-biters; and one glorious moment involving an indigo-colored Edith Head–designed gown that seems to blossom to life.

The gemstone topaz (the code name for a spy ring in the film) can be burnished in a rainbow of colors. In one essential discovery scene, Hitchcock suffused the afternoon glow with a dusty, orange-tinged amber, one of the most desirable of the topaz hue. In a film where cognac—rather than brandy—is deployed to buck up strained espionage agents (it's Paris, after all), a drink that captures both the title and Hitchcock's mise-en-scène seems appropriate.

GLASS CHAMPAGNE GLASS

1 ounce Aperol

1 ounce cognac

1 ounce lemon juice

Dash of lemon bitters

Ice

Pour all the ingredients into a shaker, stir, and strain into a champagne glass.

International spy Andre Devereaux (Frederick Stafford), embroiled in a web that also snares his wife, Nicole (Dany Robin).

ICE MAIDENS

The other woman: Judy Barton—or is it Madeleine Elster? (Kim Novak)—makes a grand entrance at Ernie's in *Vertigo* (1958).

The "Hitchcock blonde" is a familiar cinephile trope—sometimes meant in a thrilling way, sometimes in a disparaging way—although, in the end, it all comes down simply to how the director framed the "damsel in distress" within conventional Hollywood fare.

Surprising, then, to know that the first Hitchcock blonde in Hollywood was one of its most unconventional: Carole Lombard. Lombard—one of, if not simply *the* most captivating comediennes on the Hollywood scene—belonged to the small circle of intimates surrounding Hitchcock and his wife, Alma, in Los Angeles; the Hitchcocks often dined at Chasen's restaurant, where he was a weekly habitué with Lombard and her husband, Clark Gable. Lombard was desperate to make a film directed by her chum. It became Hitchcock's only comedy, *Mr. and Mrs. Smith*, and by all accounts, their badinage on the set was the highlight of Hitchcock's time on the picture. Lombard, one of the feistiest of Hitchcock's famous "blondes," was a welcome relief from the deferential heroines of his previous two or three films.

The list of Hitchcock heroines might well have included Greta Garbo. David O. Selznick, producer of *The Paradine Case*, was eager for Garbo to come out of retirement to play the (suspected) murderess, but she demurred. That's okay: it's hard to imagine anyone being more seductive (or desirable) than Alida Valli, who was brought from Italy to Hollywood, made a few pictures there (including *The Third Man*, memorably), then returned to Europe.

Hitchcock's reputation allowed him to employ the finest actors in Hollywood and in Europe, both during and after the sovereignty of the studio system, and the roll call of leading ladies who starred in his films is second to none: Ingrid Bergman, Marlene Dietrich, Grace Kelly, Doris Day, Eva Marie Saint, Kim Novak, Vera Miles, Janet Leigh, Julie Andrews, and Barbara Harris. To that list has to be added Tippi Hedren, a former model, whom Hitchcock made into a movie star after seeing her briefly in a television commercial; although Ms. Hedren took on some critical static in her day, she really steps up to the plate in *Marnie*, where she appears in practically every scene (and she was pinch-hitting for Grace Kelly, who backed out of the movie at the last minute, demurring on the notion of playing a kleptomaniac). Hedren remains the iconic Hitchcock "ice maiden."

Speaking of ice, this brings me to the best piece of advice I can give anyone who wishes to throw a sophisticated cocktail party: always get more ice than you need. However much ice you think you need, get twice as much. This way you can chill your glasses too, and, even better, you can make mistakes without running—or stressing—out.

ABOVE: Major Lacy (Nigel Bruce) does his best to behave for the second Mrs. de Winter (Joan Fontaine) in *Rebecca* (1940).
BELOW: Mrs. gives Mr.'s rival a lesson in inebriation—Carole Lombard and Gene Raymond in *Mr. and Mrs. Smith* (1941).

Tony Wendice (Ray Milland, center) mixes much mischief for his wife (Grace Kelly) and his friend–and his wife's lover (Robert Cummings)–in *Dial M for Murder* (1954).

The household staff at Manderley greets its master (Laurence Olivier) and its new mistress (Joan Fontaine).

104 | ICE MAIDENS

INSPIRED BY
REBECCA (1940)

MANDERLEY PUNCH

When Jack Favell—bounder *extraordinaire*—commands to the barman, "You might bring me a large brandy and soda. How about you, Max? Have one on me—I feel I can afford to play host," in actor George Sanders's mellifluous baritone, with the resonance of a cello and the breeziness of a golf swing, it sounds like the tastiest drink in the world.

Set on two vastly different coasts—the sun-splashed splendor of Monte Carlo and the craggy corniches of Cornwall—*Rebecca* offers up dual worlds of privilege and protocol, both of which provide a pressed-against-the-glass perspective for its unnamed heroine. The viewer also feels like an outsider, desperate to master (or even comprehend) the rituals and the affected pretentious of the upper-class gentry who populate the landscape of the de Winter family estate, Manderley.

In this context, the idea of throwing a costume ball at Manderley—the first in several years since the eponymous Rebecca was alive—requires a certain amount of guts. Our heroine provides it in spades, screwing her courage to the sticking place with her detailed preparations—meticulously re-created costume and all—centered around an enormous punch bowl providing refreshment for the local elite. That the evening itself ends on an unexpectedly unnerving note—several, in fact—is part and parcel of the spell cast by *Rebecca*.

GLASS PUNCH BOWL WITH CUPS (12)

4 ounces sugar

2 ounces grenadine syrup

64 ounces Champagne or sparkling wine

32 ounces sparkling water

8 ounces brandy

8 ounces Canton ginger liqueur

8 ounces Luxardo Maraschino liqueur

8 ounces Cointreau or orange liqueur

3 cups cracked ice

Add all the ingredients to a punch bowl and stir gently. Make sure the ice is replenished. You can also add various fruits of the season, sliced as you wish.

INSPIRED BY
REBECCA (1940)

THE DANNY

The second Mrs. de Winter could surely use a friend. She certainly doesn't find one in Manderley's housekeeper, Mrs. Danvers—or Danny, as Jack Favell sardonically calls her. Either way, she is a tall drink of water, and a dark one. Judith Anderson made an indelible impression on moviegoers as Danvers and was nominated for an Oscar as Best Supporting Actress. The depth of Anderson's obsessive commemoration of Rebecca, the first Mrs. de Winter, is terrifying, perverse, and even admirable in its way; let's raise a toast to this, er, devoted servant.

GLASS PILSNER

2 ounces brandy

1 ounce amaro

1 ounce Cherry Heering

Dash of orange bitters

Dash of walnut bitters

Ice

Add all the ingredients to a shaker, shake, and strain into a Pilsner glass.

Judith Anderson (right) as Mrs. Danvers convinces the new Mrs. de Winter (Joan Fontaine) that it's hard to get good help.

**INSPIRED BY
MR. AND MRS. SMITH (1941)**

THE EYEDROPPER

With this film—surely his most uncharacteristic—Hitchcock offers up a mildly successful screwball comedy, which is fine: after all, what kind of espionage thriller would Preston Sturges have made? *Mr. and Mrs. Smith* was inspired by the landlord of Hitchcock's rented house in Bel Air, who just happened to be Carole Lombard.

The comedy borrows a lot from Noël Coward's *Private Lives*, with its mildly risqué notion of a married couple who discover they're not legally married. Roistering among the privileged set in New York City allowed Hitchcock to cover a fair amount of drinking—in fact, one of the opening tracking shots is a veritable no-man's-land of empty liquor bottles, cocktail shakers, and drained martini glasses, the consequence of a five-day battle between the Smiths (Mr. Smith was played by Robert Montgomery). The director shrugged and admitted that this wasn't a circle of folks with whom he had much experience or much in common.

In one scene, out of spite, the "former" Mrs. Smith tries to seduce her husband's handsome law partner, but he avers his own temperance by claiming he's only tasted "an eyedropper of liquor." In response, Lombard hoists a large glass of whiskey and tells him, "This isn't alcohol, it's medicine! It kills the germs."

GLASS HIGHBALL

3 ounces bourbon

Ice

1 eyedropper of sweet vermouth

1 eyedropper of dry vermouth

1 ounce soda or seltzer

Lemon twist

Pour the bourbon into a shaker and add the ice, then the droppers of vermouth; shake and pour into a highball glass (include the ice). Add a floater of soda. (Additional points if you can get seltzer from a siphon.) Garnish with a lemon twist.

Robert Montgomery and Carole Lombard set a new standard (a rather low one) for marital discord as Mr. and Mrs. Smith.

ICE MAIDENS | 109

INSPIRED BY
THE PARADINE CASE (1947)

IN THE DOCK

The Paradine Case, set in London right after the war, churns up a reliable Hitchcock trope: a man caught between duty and desire. In this case, as it were, Gregory Peck plays a celebrated London barrister who appears dutiful in his dogged way to a fault. Alas, for him (and his loyal wife), desire in this case is embodied by Alida Valli (billed, tantalizingly, only as "Valli"), playing an inscrutable widow accused of murdering her blind husband. Although hired to defend her in the dock as a paragon of professional rectitude, Peck doesn't stand a chance. It's clear from the way Valli is photographed that Hitchcock—in addition to Peck's character—was infatuated with her; you will be, too.

If this cocktail were served with some hors d'oeuvres, it would be most appropriate to conjure up some prosciutto, as three of Hollywood's biggest hambones have significant supporting roles: Charles Coburn, brandishing a monocle and a constant state of outrage; Charles Laughton, as a port-totting, double-dealing judge; and Ethel Barrymore, as his querulous wife. Most of Barrymore's performance wound up on the cutting room floor, but apparently Academy Award judges viewed an early cut of the picture and gave her a nomination for Best Supporting Actress nonetheless.

GLASS CORDIAL

2 ounces ruby port

1 ounce Calvados

3 dashes of walnut bitters

Ice

Orange peel

Pour the liquid ingredients into a cocktail shaker with ice, shake, and strain into a cordial glass. Garnish with an orange peel.

Maddalena Paradine (Alida Valli) stares down her accusers in the Old Bailey's dock.

Lady Horfield and her husband, Judge Horfield (Ethel Barrymore and Charles Laughton), share a postprandial displeasure.

**INSPIRED BY
DIAL M FOR MURDER (1954)**

M FOR MUDDLER

There are lots of **M**s in *Dial M for Murder*: **M**aida Vale (the London neighborhood with the "M" phone exchange), **m**arriage, **m**oney, **m**anipulation, **m**ethodology, **M**argot (the potential victim), **M**ark (the lover), even **m**artinis: "Tony, don't make that martini too watery," warns Margot to her duplicitous husband, Tony Wendice (played by Ray **M**illand), who **m**asterminds the **m**odel **m**urder.

In its day, *Dial M for Murder* brought a lot of elements right side up for Hitchcock. It was his first film with Grace Kelly; it was based on a stage thriller by Frederick Knott that had been extremely successful on the West End and on Broadway; it was filmed in the then-in-vogue gimmick of 3-D (though not widely released as such); and it was a big hit, making something like thirty times its (rather contained) budget.

The bar in Tony Wendice's apartment is one of the best appointed in all of Hitchcock's films; in fact, we open in the middle of an informal cocktail party among Tony, Margot, and Mark: "Let me get you another drink" is the first line of the picture. Rather brilliantly, the bar contains a wide variety of liquor bottles at the top of the film; later on, some weeks later, when Tony is contemplating leaving town, the number of bottles is notably cut down. Still, one bottle of Johnnie Walker Red remains—just enough for one very tall and very necessary drink.

GLASS LOWBALL

1 large bunch of **M**int

1 ounce **M**andarine Napoleon liqueur

1 ounce **M**onkey 47 gin

Ice

1 ounce **M**ineral water

In a cocktail shaker, shred and rip the mint leaves to open them up. Add the liqueur. With a muddler, mash up the leaves so there's a kind of pulpy syrup. Add the gin and ice; stir and strain (a little trace of leaves is just fine) into a lowball glass; add more ice and then the mineral water. Stir gently and serve.

A poster for *Dial M for Murder*.

ICE MAIDENS | 113

INSPIRED BY
VERTIGO (1958)

THE CARLOTTA

"You go to my head / And you linger like a haunting refrain /And I find you spinning round in my brain, / Like the bubbles in a glass of Champagne . . ." So goes the old standard from the late 1930s. If ever there was a Hitchcock film that embodied that type of intoxication, it's *Vertigo*.

Vertigo hadn't been seen by a generation of filmgoers because of some bothersome litigation, and when it returned to theaters in 1985, critics and audiences went dizzy with their praise. Certainly, it's the best example of an obsession running headlong into a pathology, as Jimmy Stewart, a retired investigator with a fear of heights, falls head over heels for a doubleheader of Kim Novak in various (and shifting) guises.

Several crucial scenes are set in Ernie's, a legendary San Francisco restaurant with maroon silk brocade walls, crystal chandeliers, and deft waiters in tuxedos, serving crepes Suzette and baked Alaska. "It was like a Victorian stage setting of a high style," a Bay Area reporter once wrote. When it came time to make *Vertigo*, Ernie's was actually re-created brick by brick on a Hollywood soundstage and its owner, Victor Gotti, was sent for: "Hitchcock gave me a line in the movie," Victor recalled. "I was supposed to say 'Good evening' to Jimmy Stewart when he came into the restaurant. So he walked in and I said, 'Good evening, Mr. Stewart.' They had to shoot it again."

So, along with ordering drinks at Ernie's you can mold yourself a Carlotta, using tequila and green crème de menthe—the Mexican background and the color scheme should work.

Of course, you'd have to make it a double.

GLASS CORDIAL

1½ ounces white tequila

1½ ounces green crème de menthe

Ice

Flower (optional)

In a cocktail shaker, mix the tequila, crème de menthe, and ice, and then strain into a cordial glass. Garnish with a flower, if desired.

A poster for *Vertigo*.

114 | ICE MAIDENS

INSPIRED BY
MARNIE (1964)

THE FORIO

Marnie confounds both Hitchcock enthusiasts and detractors; certainly contemporary mores make some of its suppositions difficult to endorse. That said, it is a compelling psychological mystery with some bravura sequences, an Ibsen play directed as if it were a heist picture.

Tippi Hedren as the eponymous heroine manages several difficult tasks—not only is she onscreen almost all the time, but she is also compelling and cool, like a blonde kleptomaniac locked-room puzzle with equine skills and equipoise. (The only mammal she trusts is her horse, Forio.) As the scion of a wealthy Maryland family, Sean Connery—who filmed this in between his first two engagements as James Bond—exhibits his own psychological complexity. His character, Mark Rutland, seems to find rejection and reticence particularly arousing.

Given the elevated social stratosphere of Mark and his class, there is, of course, a more-than-sufficient amount of social drinking, cocktail parties, and so on. Brandy and bourbon appear to be the solution to any problem: "Would you like some bourbon to brush your teeth?" asks Mark of Marnie on their honeymoon, hoping to mediate her intractability.

This cocktail highlights a psychological clue to Marnie's deep, dark past; a couple of them might lead you to reveal a few secrets as well . . .

GLASS LOWBALL

1½ ounces vodka

1 ounce Cherry Heering liqueur

Dash of Luxardo bitters

1 ounce grenadine syrup

Ice

Brandied cherry (if you can avoid the radioactive red ones, great)

Place the liquid ingredients in a shaker with ice; shake and strain into a lowball glass. Skewer a cherry on a toothpick or mini-skewer and add to the drink.

Beset by complications both internal and external, Tippi Hedren's Marnie is the embodiment of retribution.

ICE MAIDENS | 117

NAME YOUR POISON

Secret agent Devlin (Cary Grant) tries to steer Ingrid Bergman's dissolute Alicia Huberman on the path to redemption in *Notorious* (1946).

Tangmere-by-the-Sea, where most of *Suspicion* is set, seems to be your typical quaint Cornish seaside town: it's got a local pub and a postbox and its very own murder mystery author—don't most quaint English towns?

Isobel Sedbusk (played charmingly by Auriol Lee, who, tragically, was killed in a car accident before the film's release) appears wise beyond her avocation—she seems to know her poisons quite well and is more than willing to share her expertise at the dinner table (she also seems to have, if you look carefully, a female partner—a relationship rarely even hinted at in a Hollywood movie). As she tells the heroine (and potential victim), Lina:

> **Isobel:** Imagine a substance in daily use everywhere. Anyone can lay his hands on it, and within a minute after taking, the victim's beautifully out of the way. Mind you, it's undetectable after death.
>
> **Lina:** Is whatever it is, painful?
>
> **Isobel:** Oh, not in the least. In fact, I should think it'd be a most pleasant death.

Sedbusk's character is, perhaps, a takeoff on mystery author Agatha Christie, a Hitchcock contemporary who also lived in a quaint English town. Christie used poison to knock off nearly half of the victims in her novels and was trained by a pharmacist, so she knew quite a lot about their variety and efficacy.

Throughout Hitchcock's films, there's the conviviality of drinking in various middle-class rituals, such as Champagne toasts, dinner parties, and postprandial chats by the fireside. They are, of course, deceptive; in *Shadow of a Doubt*, Uncle Charlie's most nihilistic speech is given right at the dinner table—over a nice glass of wine. It's a different kind of poisoning—a kind of moral toxin—but no less effective. Even after-dinner coffee might prove detrimental to one's health; poor Alicia (played by Ingrid Bergman) in *Notorious* experiences a slow kind of disorientation and demise over countless cups of espresso, poured solicitously by her poisoners, as if they would actually be salubrious instead.

All of which is to say, even with the sociability and whimsy of these Hitchcocktails, please drink responsibly.

OPPOSITE: Johnnie's (Cary Grant) moral ambiguity is the narrative center of *Suspicion* (here with Joan Fontaine as his wife, Lina).
ABOVE: Uncle Charlie (Joseph Cotten), the serial murderer in *Shadow of a Doubt* (1943), enjoys a rare respite before he has to take it on the lam–again.
BELOW: Alicia (Ingrid Bergman), following orders, charms the besotted Alex Sebastian (Claude Rains) in *Notorious* (1946).

Hack psychic Madame Blanche (Barbara Harris) and her out-of-work actor boyfriend (Bruce Dern) plot a roadside diversion in *Family Plot* (1976).

INSPIRED BY
***SUSPICION* (1941)**

MONKEY FACE

"What's in this drink?" is a perfectly reasonable question, asked by imbibers by the thousands every single day. In no other Hitchcock movie, however, does the question seem so pertinent.

Suspicion is notable for several factors: Joan Fontaine, as the querulous, inquisitive heroine Lina; the director's first team-up with Cary Grant as the irrepressible Johnnie Aysgarth; and the seemingly bloody-minded waffling on the film's conclusion. The last two aspects are inextricably wrapped up in each other: Grant, easily the most charming actor in Hollywood, couldn't possibly be a homicidal bounder, could he? Hence the zigs and zags of the film's final scenes.

Still, the British setting (re-created in Hollywood, of course) offers us many well-stocked bars and hunt club balls at which to enjoy some sophisticated drinking. Grant's pal, Beaky, played by Nigel Bruce, is particularly enthusiastic about a bracing drink or two; a particular bet involving a large glass of brandy might well be his undoing.

The threat of poisoning was abetted by Hitchcock's own meddling with one particular mixture: he supposedly added a flashlight bulb inside a glass of milk, allowing it to pull focus for his purposes.

GLASS HIGHBALL

Submersible LED mini-light

1 ounce brandy

1 ounce crème de banane liqueur

1 ounce heavy cream

Crushed ice

Ground nutmeg

Turn on the LED light and place it at the bottom of the highball glass. In a cocktail shaker, combine the brandy, liqueur, heavy cream, and crushed ice. Shake, then gently strain into the glass. Top with a sprinkle of ground nutmeg.

Joan Fontaine–the very embodiment of *Suspicion*.

Charlie (Teresa Wright) cornered by her namesake, Uncle Charlie (Joseph Cotten), has all of her fears about him confirmed.

INSPIRED BY
SHADOW OF A DOUBT (1943)

MERRY WIDOW

Even though it is set at the advent of World War II in a charming small town in Northern California, *Shadow of a Doubt* feels as if it were the most Victorian of Hitchcock's films. Perhaps it is the gingerbread architecture of Santa Rosa, or the cozy feeling of family values and small-town rituals, or the delicate but distinctive hand of Thornton Wilder's work on the screenplay.

The Merry Widow certainly plays a part in that atmosphere. Although Joseph Cotten's duplicitous serial killer, Charlie Oakley, has earned a reputation as the "Merry Widow Murderer," that's not an arbitrary denotative moniker. *The Merry Widow* was an operetta by the Viennese composer Franz Lehár; written in 1904, it took the world by storm and every living room parlor in Europe and America would have had the sheet music to "The Merry Widow Waltz" perched on its piano. In fact, Hitchcock memorializes the music's popularity with his credit sequence of swirling couples waltzing to the tune.

Couples, duality, and duplicity are, as critics have pointed out, central to Hitchcock's immaculate design of the movie (and what is a shadow, after all, but a second self?). Uncle Charlie's affinity for his niece is reflected in her name: Charlie. There's an intense showdown between the two Charlies in the Til-Two Club, where Uncle Charlie orders—wait for it—a double brandy.

GLASS COUPE OR MARTINI

1¼ ounces oloroso sherry

1 ounce brandy

½ ounce orange juice

1 teaspoon cola syrup

Ice

Dash of ground cinnamon

Add the liquid ingredients with ice to a cocktail shaker. Shake and strain into a coupe. Sprinkle a dash of cinnamon on top.

The Newton family, tripping down memory lane (l-r: Patricia Collinge, Teresa Wright, Joseph Cotten, Henry Travers, Charles Bates, and Edna May Wonacott).

NAME YOUR POISON | 127

INSPIRED BY
NOTORIOUS (1946)

THE COCOPIRINHA

In his films previous to *Notorious*, Hitchcock either had a first-rate male movie star (Joseph Cotten, Cary Grant) or a first-rate female movie star (Carole Lombard, Ingrid Bergman). Finally, the stars aligned, as it were, and, with the exhilaratingly sexual tension between Grant and Bergman, a first-rate movie emerged. *Notorious* is part espionage film, part romance, and a surprisingly adult movie at a historical moment when postwar cinema begins to elbow against the restraints of the studio system.

The act of drinking can be traced through the narrative of *Notorious* like a snake slithering through the Brazilian jungle. The film's second scene is a raucous party ("The important drinking hasn't started yet") led by Ingrid Bergman as a woman with a dubious reputation. That leads to a hair-raising inebriated drive through Miami, followed by one giant hangover visited upon Bergman's character, Alicia. Following a flight to Rio de Janeiro, a secret mission ensues, as well as an incipient romance between Bergman and Grant, celebrated with a bottle of Champagne—a bottle that gets misplaced when the romantic relationship gets waylaid in lieu of duty. Then it's on to a round of martinis with the suave villain (embodied touchingly by Claude Rains); an extravagant cocktail party for Rio's Nazi-minded elite where the liquor may just run out; a scavenger hunt in a wine cellar; and a series of slow poisonings, courtesy of a jealous mother and some elegant espresso cups.

The supreme achievement of *Notorious* (this author's favorite Hitchcock film) earns it three cocktail recipes. This first one is a celebration of the caipirinha, the national drink of Brazil. As Grant and Bergman's plane begins its descent to Rio, the sexual tension is already in the air; raise a glass to the exotic locale and the beginning of an enthrallingly complex relationship.

GLASS LOWBALL

1 lime, cut into quarters

1 teaspoon fine sugar

2 ounces cachaça

1 ounce Clément coconut liqueur

Ice

Coconut flakes

Place the lime quarters and sugar at the bottom of the lowball glass. Use a muddler to get as much juice out of them as possible. Add the cachaça, liqueur, and ice. Place half of a Boston shaker around the glass and shake vigorously. Add some coconut flakes on top.

INSPIRED BY
NOTORIOUS (1946)

MADAME SEBASTIAN

We now raise a glass to the supremely gifted Austrian actress Leopoldine Konstantin in her only Hollywood movie, playing the nefarious mother of Claude Rains's overly sentimental Nazi spy (she was only three years older than Rains). Strictly business—and, in her own way, as infatuated with her son as he is with Ingrid Bergman—Madame Sebastian mixes a mean cup of espresso. For the film, one of those cups was giant-sized and built by the studio props department so Hitchcock could shoot it in the foreground and still have Ingrid Bergman in focus.

GLASS CORDIAL
(OR EVEN AN ESPRESSO CUP)

2 ounces Mr. Black coffee liqueur

1 ounce brandy

1 large ice cube

Dash of heavy cream

Simple syrup (optional)

In a cocktail shaker, stir the brandy and coffee liqueur together; pour over a large ice cube in a cordial glass, then add a dash of heavy cream. (You may add some simple syrup if you like.) Do not stir.

THE HANGOVER

In a movie filled with inventive shots, perhaps none is so imaginative (and witty) as Alicia's first glimpse of secret agent Devlin on the morning after an evening of binge drinking; she sees him upside down, framed in the doorway of her bedroom. Hitchcock swivels the camera 180 degrees as Cary Grant proffers Bergman some sort of ghastly remedy and some advice: "You'd better drink this—finish it."

GLASS HIGHBALL

Note: This is a nonalcoholic drink.

4 ounces coconut water

6 ounces orange juice

1 ounce honey

1½ teaspoons baking soda

Pinch of salt

A little bit of ice

Place all the ingredients in a blender, or if you don't have one, place them in a sealed container, shake vigorously, and refrigerate for 30 minutes (if you can wait that long). Pour into a highball glass.

ABOVE: Devlin and Alicia (Cary Grant and Ingrid Bergman) hoping the Champagne won't run out, under the keen eye of fellow party guest Señora Ortiz (Lenore Ulric).

FOLLOWING PAGES: If your mother-in-law thinks you're a spy, never let her make you espresso: poisoned peril in a coffee cup. Ingrid Bergman in *Notorious*.

INSPIRED BY
FAMILY PLOT (1976)

MADAME BLANCHE

Hitchcock's final film is set in a purposefully indistinct universe of Northern California signposts: freeways, malls, bungalows, gas stations, burger joints, jewelry stores. And a graveyard, too. It looks like every 1970s television drama you've ever seen. This is to provide a quotidian background for the tale of two separate plots—as it were—of mischief and chicanery, the hidden scams and swindles that probably go on behind closed doors in every small town in America.

The director never quite got the cast he was hoping for—Liza Minnelli and Jack Nicholson's names were bandied about—and that might have helped give the movie more octane. But the two pairs of schemers who wind up crossing paths to potentially lethal effect are more than sufficient: Barbara Harris and Bruce Dern as a (seemingly) fake psychic and her cab driver boyfriend; then, William Devane and Karen Black as a pair of suburban kidnappers, resourceful enough to have a secret cell in their garage where they can hide their victims and yet civil enough to offer them a nice Italian meal with a decent wine.

Alas, they are also devious enough to wield a hypodermic needle filled with a strong sedative when necessary, which gives us the poison of the chapter title. Luckily, Barbara Harris proves prescient enough to think ahead; as the ambiguously paranormal Madame Blanche, her psychic powers seem to hide in plain sight . . .

GLASS LOWBALL

1 ounce dry vermouth

1 ounce grappa

1 ounce Canton ginger liqueur

Rock-candy swizzle stick

Add the vermouth, grappa, and Canton liqueur to a cocktail shaker and shake. Pour the mixture into a lowball glass and stir three times with the rock-candy swizzle stick. Set the swizzle stick aside for later; you don't want the drink to be too sweet.

Madame Blanche (Barbara Harris, right) attempts to pull a psychic veil over her mark, Julia Rainbird (Cathleen Nesbitt).

NAME YOUR POISON | 135

INSPIRED BY HITCHCOCK FILMS

THE MACGUFFIN

The MacGuffin has become a legendary and somewhat misunderstood concept. It's not a fake and it's not a meaningless thing in and of itself—as Hitchcock once said, "It's the thing the spies are after, but the audience doesn't care." The *spies* care about it and the people who get in the *way* of the spies care about it, but, true, the audience members, upon leaving the cinema, would not do too well on a "MacGuffin" quiz.

In an address at Columbia University, during his first visit to America in 1939 (and before he set foot in Hollywood), Hitchcock gave another answer:

"It might be a Scottish name, taken from a story about two men on a train. One man says, 'What's that package up there in the baggage rack?' And the other answers, 'Oh, that's a MacGuffin.' The first one asks, 'What's a MacGuffin?' 'Well,' the other man says, 'it's an apparatus for trapping lions in the Scottish Highlands.' The first man says, 'But there are no lions in the Scottish Highlands,' and the other one answers, 'Well, then, that's no MacGuffin!' So you see that a MacGuffin is actually nothing at all."

In our case, a MacGuffin is a drink in a cocktail book with no alcohol at all.

GLASS HIGHBALL

---

3 ounces Topo Chico lime mint soda

½ ounce lime juice

2 dashes grenadine

Ice

Sprig of mint

Add the soda, lime juice, grenadine, and ice to a highball glass and mix gently. Garnish with a sprig of mint. By all means, pretend it's got actual booze in it.

OPPOSITE: What's in that wine bottle, really? Uranium, actually—but it hardly matters: Ingrid Bergman and Cary Grant in *Notorious*.
FOLLOWING PAGES: Dead drunk: well, dead anyway... *The Trouble with Harry*.

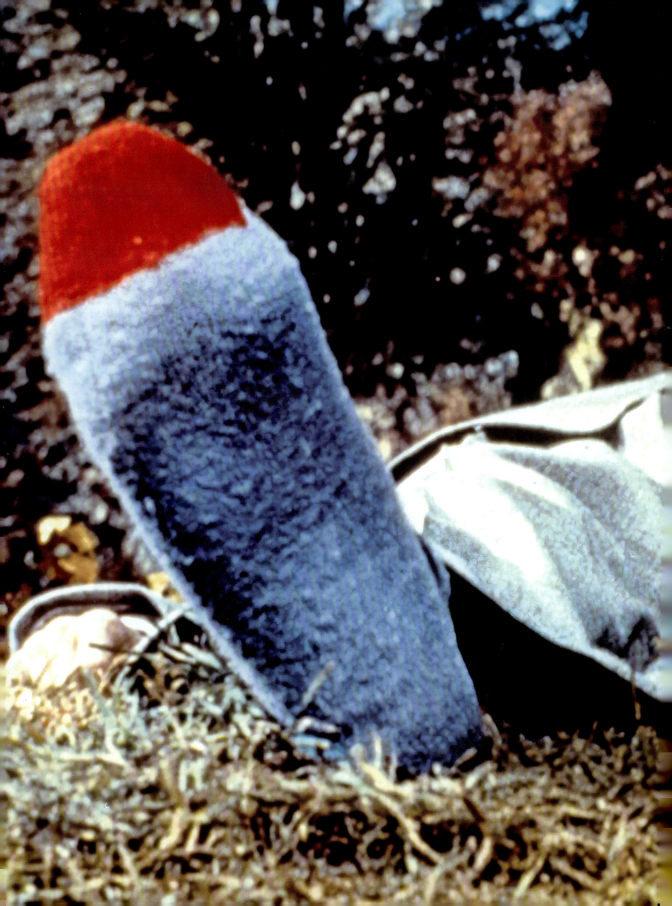

LIST OF DRINKS

BY MAIN INGREDIENT

BOURBON

Avez Vous, *To Catch a Thief* [page 92]

The Eyedropper, *Mr. and Mrs. Smith* [page 109]

George Kaplan, *North by Northwest* [page 30]

Miss Lonelyhearts, *Rear Window* [page 51]

BRANDY

The Danny, *Rebecca* [page 106]

Monkey Face, *Suspicion* [page 124]

The Savoy Hotel Cocktail, *Foreign Correspondent* [page 44]

CACHAÇA

The Cocopirinha, *Notorious* [page 128]

CHAMPAGNE

Manderley Punch, *Rebecca* [page 105]

The Rushmore, *North by Northwest* [page 28]

COFFEE LIQUEUR

Madame Sebastian, *Notorious* [page 130]

COGNAC

The Topaz, *Topaz* [page 96]

GIN

The Cameo [page 73]

Clause 27, *Foreign Correspondent* [page 47]

Criss Cross (Drink 1), *Strangers on a Train* [page 74]

Gin and French, *The Man Who Knew Too Much* [page 20]

Lovely Ducks, *Stage Fright* [page 24]

M for Muddler, *Dial M for Murder* [page 113]

The Stork Club Cocktail, *The Wrong Man* [page 27]

Test Match, *The Lady Vanishes* [page 64]

Vanishing Lady, *The Lady Vanishes* [page 67]

LILLET

Corpse Reviver No. 8, *The Trouble with Harry* [page 95]

Maquis Mouse, *To Catch a Thief* [page 91]

The Rosie, *Lifeboat* [page 84]

PORT
In the Dock, *The Paradine Case* [page 110]

RUM
Shrunken Head, *Under Capricorn* [page 87]

SCOTCH
Gabriel Valley, *Spellbound* [page 69]

SHERRY
Merry Widow, *Shadow of a Doubt* [page 127]

Que Sera, *The Man Who Knew Too Much* [page 52]

TEQUILA
The Carlotta, *Vertigo* [page 114]

The General, *Secret Agent* [page 43]

La Paloma, *The Birds* [page 33]

Mrs. Oxford's Margarita, *Frenzy* [page 34]

VERMOUTH
Madame Blanche, *Family Plot* [page 135]

VODKA
A Boy's Best Friend, *Psycho* [page 77]

Criss Cross (Drink 2), *Strangers on a Train* [page 74]

The Forio, *Marnie* [page 117]

The Gibson, *North by Northwest* [page 30]

The Tivolini, *Torn Curtain* [page 55]

WHISKY
Alt-Na-Shellach, *The 39 Steps* [page 23]

Cock Robin, *Sabotage* [page 62]

The Frontenac, *I Confess* [page 88]

Route 66, *Saboteur* [page 48]

Tied Together, *Rope* [page 70]

NON-ALCOHOLIC
The Hangover, *Notorious* [page 130]

The MacGuffin [page 136]

ACKNOWLEDGMENTS

It's not often—if ever—that a book proposal gets accepted on the basis of a one-word title, but such is the acuity and receptiveness of editor Karyn Gerhard that all she had to hear was "Hitchcocktails" and she knew immediately what I was after. Karyn is a paradigm of editorial taste and discretion and I'm thrilled that, after our successful collaboration on the previous Weldon Owen book, *I'll Drink to That!*, she took this one on and has steered it so effortlessly into harbor.

Joan Marcus has again proven to be the best possible collaborator as well, turning her theatrical talents toward the world of legendary cinema by training her camera lens toward Hitchcock. Much gratitude to Joan for our second book and I hope this work continues to be an inspiration for her (and thanks to Adrian Bryan-Brown for allowing us to turn his home into a studio deluged with eccentric concoctions and to Amy Klein for her invaluable contributions during our photo shoots).

Genevieve Elam and Miles Maslon supportively suffered under the many experiments conducted in our kitchen, bar, and living room; kudos also to those eager taste-testers Linus and Eileen Hume; Cameron and Tim Rice, Albert Cuadra and Tracey Arnell; Matthew Sussman and Angie Lieber. (Matt was also a consistent and reliable sounding board.) Gordon Bean worked his usual magic with an inspired notion for the book's final cocktail.

Thanks to my agent Steve Ross and a doff of the shower curtain to Mark Shanahan, whose love for the Master of Suspense provided endless inspiration (and countless puns).

And, finally, gratitude to the master himself, Alfred Hitchcock, for a body of work that is so endlessly enjoyable, exploitable, and effervescent.

ABOUT THE PHOTOGRAPHER

Joan Marcus is one of the preeminent theatrical photographers working in the US today. Over the past 25 years she has photographed more than 500 shows on and off Broadway and regionally. A native of Pittsburgh, Pennsylvania, Joan graduated from George Washington University. In 2014 she received a Tony Honor for Excellence in the Theater. She was also the photographer for *I'll Drink to That! Broadway's Legendary Stars, Shows, and the Cocktails They Inspired.*

ABOUT THE AUTHOR

Laurence Maslon is an arts professor in the Graduate Acting Program at New York University's Tisch School of the Arts. His most recent books are *I'll Drink to That! Broadway's Legendary Stars, Shows, and the Cocktails They Inspired* (Gold Medal winner, IBPA Awards), and an updated companion volume to the PBS series *Broadway: The American Musical*. He is also the host and producer of the weekly radio series, *Broadway to Main Street* (winner of the 2019 ASCAP Foundation/Deems Taylor Award for Radio Broadcast) on the NPR station WLIW-FM. Other books include the companion book to *Come From Away*; *Broadway to Main Street: How Show Music Enchanted America* (Oxford); *The Sound of Music Companion*; and the *South Pacific Companion*. He is the writer and coproducer of the PBS American Masters documentary, *Sammy Davis, Jr.: I've Gotta Be Me*, and wrote the *American Masters* documentary *Richard Rodgers: The Sweetest Sounds*. He served on the nominating committee for the Tony Awards from 2007 to 2010. He has written for *The New York Times*, *The Washington Post*, the *New Yorker*, *Opera News*, *Stagebill*, and *American Theatre*. Mr. Maslon, otherwise a nice guy, mixes a mean drink.

The author at Old Westbury Gardens, one of the filming locations for *North by Northwest*.

weldonowen

an imprint of Insight Editions
P.O. Box 3088
San Rafael, CA 94912
www.weldonowen.com

To Mark Shanahan—a boy's best friend—
after his mother, of course.

CEO Raoul Goff
VP, Publisher Roger Shaw
Senior Editor Karyn Gerhard
Editorial Assistant Jon Ellis
VP Creative Chrissy Kwasnik
Designer Megan Sinead Bingham
Production Designer Jean Hwang
VP Manufacturing Alix Nicholaeff
Senior Production Manager Joshua Smith
Strategic Production Planner Lina s Palma-Temena

Cocktail Photography by Joan Marcus
All film images courtesy the Everett Collection, with the exception of the following: Imago: 7; Masheter Movie Archive/Alamy Stock Photo: 11; Photofest: 4, 17 (top), 18-19, 33, 38, 39 (bottom), 50, 51, 60-61, 70, 81 (bottom), 82-83, 84, 88, 101 (top), 102-103, 111.
Author photo by Matthew Sussman

Weldon Owen would also like to thank Karen Levy, Amy Klein, and Margaret Parrish for their work on this book.

Text © 2025 Laurence Maslon

All rights reserved. No part of this book may be reproduced in any form without written permission from the publisher.

ISBN: 979-8-88674-219-0

Manufactured in China by Insight Editions
10 9 8 7 6 5 4 3 2 1

Insight Editions, in association with Roots of Peace, will plant two trees for each tree used in the manufacturing of this book. Roots of Peace is an internationally renowned humanitarian organization dedicated to eradicating land mines worldwide and converting war-torn lands into productive farms and wildlife habitats. Roots of Peace will plant two million fruit and nut trees in Afghanistan and provide farmers there with the skills and support necessary for sustainable land use.

PAGE 2: In *Suspicion* (1941), Johnnie Aysgarth (Cary Grant) brings a libation to his bride. What's in the glass is both a narrative and a cinematic secret.